Perfect Wood Finishing Made Easy

Perfect Wood Finishing

MADE EASY

Sue Noble

POPULAR WOODWORKING BOOKS
CINCINNATI, OHIO

ABOUT THE AUTHOR

Sue Noble has been finishing wood professionally for eighteen years. Her experiences range from a small refinishing shop to a large custom millwork manufacturing company. She has taught wood finishing clinics and authored finishing guides for woodworkers. Sue and her partner, Bill Lindenschmidt, have owned and operated Noble Finishing in Cincinnati, Ohio for ten years.

Perfect Wood Finishing Made Easy. Copyright © 1998 by Susanne M. Noble. Manufactured in China. All rights reserved. No part of this book may be reproduced in any form or by any electronic or mechanical means including information storage and retrieval systems without permission in writing from the publisher, except by a reviewer, who may quote brief passages in a review. Published by Popular Woodworking Books, an imprint of F&W Publications, Inc., 1507 Dana Avenue, Cincinnati, Ohio 45207. (800) 289-0963. First edition.

Other fine Popular Woodworking Books are available from your local bookstore or direct from the publisher.

02 01 00 99 98   5 4 3 2 1

Library of Congress Cataloging-in-Publication Data

Noble, Susanne M.
    Perfect wood finishing made easy / by Susanne M. Noble.
        p.   cm.
    Includes index.
    ISBN 1-55870-460-4 (pb: alk. paper)
    1. Wood finishing. I. Title.
TT325.N63   1998
683.1′043—dc21   97-38046
                                                            CIP

Editor: R. Adam Blake
Production editor: Marilyn Daiker
Interior designer: Sandy Conopeotis Kent
Cover designer: Chad Planner

Special thanks to the following craftsmen and designers: Charlie Ehlers for the cherry shaker table; Keith Mealy for the curly maple CD box; for the pine TV/stereo cabinet, Jonathan J. Johnson, with the design by Anne W. Chatfield, ASID allied; Dan Kreimer for the walnut box; and James Stuard for the briefcase.

READ THIS IMPORTANT SAFETY NOTICE

To prevent accidents, keep safety in mind while you work. Use the safety guards installed on power equipment, keep fingers away from saw blades, wear safety goggles to prevent injuries from flying wood chips and sawdust, wear headphones to protect your hearing, and consider installing a dust vacuum to reduce the amount of airborne sawdust in your woodshop. Don't wear loose clothing, such as neckties or shirts with loose sleeves, or jewelry, such as rings, necklaces or bracelets, when working on power equipment. The author and editors who compiled this book have tried to make all the contents as accurate and correct as possible. Plans, illustrations, photographs and text have been carefully checked. All instructions, plans and projects should be carefully read, studied and understood before beginning construction. Due to the variability of local conditions, construction materials, skill levels, etc., neither the author nor Popular Woodworking Books assumes any responsibility for any accidents, injuries, damages or other losses incurred resulting from the material presented in this book.

DEDICATION

This book is dedicated to my mom who bought me the "antiquing" kit when I was twelve that got me hooked on finishing and to Frank Coore who taught me to love the art of finishing.

ACKNOWLEDGMENTS

Thanks to:

- Sandy Warner, Bill Lindenschmidt and all my associates at Noble Finishing for their support, encouragement and input.
- Adam Blake for the photography that makes the book, and for guiding me through my first publishing experience.
- All the folks at Popular Woodworking Books and *Popular Woodworking Magazine*.

CHAPTER ONE

Rich Oil Finish on a Walnut Box

Learn the techniques that will ensure best results from simple wipe-on oil finishes.

CHAPTER TWO

Easy Gel Stain and Varnish Finish on an Oak Shelf

Gel stains are easy to apply, and add depth and consistency to splotchy woods. Learn the steps to a beautiful finish on any species of wood.

CHAPTER THREE

Beautiful Dye and Polyurethane Finish on a Cherry Table

Using a dye on a tight grained wood like cherry can enhance the natural beauty of the wood. Learn how to apply dye step by step on this cherry table.

CHAPTER FOUR

Warm Glaze and Shellac Finish on a Walnut Picture Frame

Learn how to take a new walnut frame and give it the warm patina of a beautifully aged antique.

CHAPTER FIVE

Professional Filled and Dyed Finish on a Mahogany and Sapele Briefcase

Here is everything you need to apply a durable finish on a briefcase made of wood. You'll learn how to fill open grained woods for a smooth-as-glass finish.

INTRODUCTION

There are many reasons to apply some kind of finish to wood. Most importantly, the finish protects the wood from drying out and eventually falling apart. It also protects the wood from unsightly stains and damage. But beyond its protective nature, the right finish can highlight and unleash the natural beauty of the wood, make the piece fit in better with a decorating scheme, or re-create the glow that an aged, well-cared for piece of furniture has. Finishing is part science, part craft and part art.

The science of finishing is very complicated, but extensive knowledge of it is not at all necessary to complete a beautiful project. This book gives you enough information to apply a beautiful finish without burdening you with what is happening at a molecular level. I don't understand a fraction of the science involved in making this computer I'm writing on work, but that doesn't stop me from using it. If you're interested in the science of actually making a finish, great. But for those of us who just want it to work, a little knowledge goes a long way.

The art of finishing is a little more difficult to convey in words and pictures. Art has to do with creating beauty and has to come from within. It's seeing the potential beauty of a piece of wood and making that happen.

The craft of finishing is the primary focus of this book. It is intended for those who are just being introduced to the craft, but more experienced finishers will find it useful for a fresh look at the basics.

Learning something new can be a daunting task because it seems there is so much you need to know before you even start. To make it easier to get started, this book is organized by projects that have step-by-step directions written in plain language. Only a few projects require special finishing equipment and most can be completed with supplies purchased at a local hardware or paint store. Each project includes clues about how different woods should be treated.

People are mystified by finishing because it seems to them that they can do the exact same process at two different times and have totally different results. It's not a plot. Usually the different results can be traced back to the difference between the woods, difference in environment, or difference in preparation. This is where the craft of finishing enters. There are indeed certain guidelines to follow. In this book, I talk about the characteristics of different woods and how best to deal with them. There are some simple tips to help control your finishing environment. And most importantly, a lot of instruction on the preparation of wood prior to finishing.

From my very first refinishing project, I was hooked by the immediate gratification and satisfaction of creating something beautiful. With this book you can enjoy this same satisfaction.

HOW TO USE THIS BOOK

This is an honest book. Almost every single step of each project was photographed—including the mistakes I made and what I had to do to fix them. Nothing was done off camera to make a difference in the outcome. No information or secrets have been held back from you. Here is an overview to help you get the most out of the book.

Like any finishing project, this book starts with preparation. It's the part we'd all like to skip. Unfortunately, it is by far the most important part of the finishing process. Since the steps involved in proper preparation apply to all the projects, the general directions have all been included in this section. It may not be the most fun part of the book, but please take the time to read it carefully—it could save you a lot of headaches later.

Following the preparation section are ten projects that take you step by step through the finishing process. The introduction to each project explains why I chose a particular finish for the project, unusual characteristics of a particular wood or construction, and the overall look I was trying to achieve. The projects are roughly arranged in order of simplest to most difficult. Each project uses a different type of stain and finish and explains what other combinations are possible. Suggestions for appropriate uses of each finish are given. I've also included for each project a thorough list of all the materials needed.

Included with each step is a small icon giving an approximate amount of time the step should take. Of course, these are only rough estimates and will vary greatly with your experience and with the project you are working on. However, they will let you know it shouldn't take three hours to sand the sealer coat on a small table.

In addition to the step-by-step directions, each chapter includes Tips. These can be hints specific to the project, but most often are suggestions that can be applied to all types of finishes. Sidebars explain special processes involved in the project that require more detailed information.

Every chapter concludes with suggestions for maintenance and repair of the finish used on the project.

At the back of the book you'll find a glossary defining some of the more technical terms in the book. I've tried to explain everything as I go, but this could be a handy reference. The resource list will help you track down any of the supplies used in the projects that might not be available at a local paint store. And finally, the finish characteristics and compatibility chart summarizes the solvents, dry times and application methods, and the features of different stains and finishes as well as giving a guide for using different finishes together.

This is important.

THE SECRET TO A BEAUTIFUL FINISH IS PROPER PREPARATION OF THE WOOD.

No tricks, no secret formulas, no complicated procedures—just careful, meticulous preparation. That makes this chapter the most important one in the book—and probably the one most people will skip. If you have problems with any of the projects, come back to this chapter.

The purpose of preparation is to create a surface that will accept stain and finish evenly. The projects assume the wood is ready for its final 120-grit sanding. Some people sand to finer grits than that, but a 120-grit sanding provides a reliable working surface. Sanding is actually a process of putting finer and finer scratches on the wood surface. Too coarse and they suck up finish too readily—too fine and they don't absorb at all. This chapter will discuss what needs to be done before the 120-grit sanding.

Let's begin by defining some terms.

PORE—Wood comes from trees. Pretty elementary, but important to keep in mind. Trees are made up of cells. When the wood dries, all that is left are the oval-shaped cell walls that are made up of cellulose. The empty space inside a cell is the pore.

GRAIN—Wood cells are arranged in a linear fashion. The pattern is called grain. Different species of trees have different grain patterns.

MILL MARKS, PLANER MARKS, KNIFE MARKS—As trees are turned into lumber or veneer they go through a series of saws and planers. Each of these machines will leave marks from their knives. If not removed, these marks show up as dark blotches.

CROSS-GRAIN SCRATCHES—Scratches that go against the grain of the wood tear into the cell walls making jagged edges which soak up stain and look dark and unnatural.

SWIRL MARKS—Many power sanders have pads that move in an orbital pattern. This allows them to remove a lot of material quickly, but they also tend to leave scratches that look like little squigglies.

DENT—A dent happens when pressure is applied to the cell walls and they collapse. No tearing of the walls occur, so they don't appear darker; but they do show up when finish is applied because the light reflects off of them differently than the smooth surface. Sometimes they even appear lighter because the cells have been so compressed no stain can get into the pore of the wood.

GOUGE—A gouge is a dent that has torn a cell wall by actually removing a chunk of it. The raw edges soak up stain and appear much darker than the surrounding wood.

BURNS—The friction created from a saw blade or router can literally burn the wood, creating unsightly black marks.

GLUE SPOTS—Any excess glue left on the surface seals off the grain and prevents stain and finish from being absorbed, leaving a light spot.

VENEER—Wood can be sliced very thinly and glued to another surface. This is done to create beautiful patterns, save money and resources, and provide stability. The veneer must be firmly glued to the substrate or it will bubble up.

WATER SPOTS—Because wood is made of dry cells, it acts like a sponge when water gets on it. Spots that dry and are not sanded remain very open and show up as dark spots under finish.

You Need

- cabinet scraper
- aluminum oxide sandpaper—80, 100 grit
- wood putty
- hard rubber- or cork-covered wood sanding block
- iron
- damp rag
- ½" stiff blade putty knife
- curved grapefruit putty knife
- carpenter's glue
- syringe
- wax paper
- clamps
- masking tape
- miscellaneous sandpaper

Step-by-Step Directions

STEP 1

Do most sanding before assembly. It's much easier to do an aggressive sanding when you don't have to sand into joints and corners. Place your piece on a firm surface at a comfortable working height. Sanding isn't much fun, so don't make it any harder than it has to be!

Begin sanding with 80-grit paper and a hard block. This is the time to get rid of any knife marks or saw burns. The hard block is important because it helps plane down the surface. Sandpaper held in your hand will only follow the contours of the wood, not change them.

STEP 2

After assembling the piece, fill any gouges, chips or open joints with a wood putty that is a shade lighter than your finished piece will be; it will darken when stain and finish are applied. This photo shows the open joints that need to be filled.

TIPS

Buy or make a sandpaper tearer. A roughly torn edge on a piece of sandpaper can act like a file and cut like a knife into the wood or finish. Tear the paper over a very sharp edge with the abrasive side up. The smooth edge of an old hacksaw blade is great for ripping.

STEP 3

Try not to get putty where it doesn't belong—it will fill in the pores of the wood. Even if you sand the surface clean, a light spot will show because stain won't be evenly absorbed.

STEP 4

Let the putty dry hard before proceeding—it will dry to a much lighter color. To tell if it is dry, press with your fingernail—no dent should show.

STEP 5

Completely sand off all excess putty. Only the putty that is actually in the joint, dent or hole should remain. Sometimes putty shrinks up and when dry is not level with the surface. Apply more putty and repeat the sanding process.

STEP 6

Sand the assembled piece with 100-grit paper. All sanding should be done with, not against, the grain of the wood—even into corners and miter joints. Use a hard sanding block where possible.

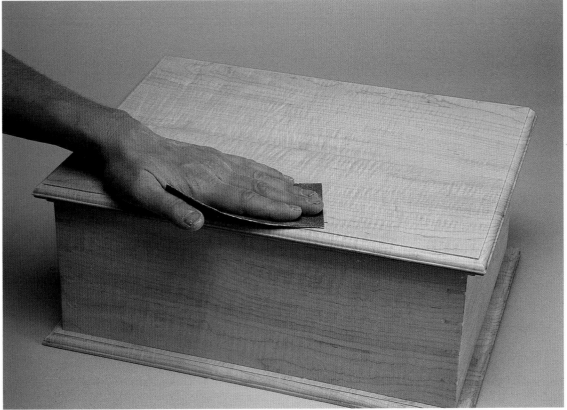

STEP 7

On smaller surfaces tear a sheet of sandpaper in half and fold in thirds to make a sanding pad. Sand out any cross-grain scratches. If you use a power sander, don't force the machine by applying too much pressure. This will slow the motor down and leave deeper sanding scratches. When using an orbital sander, it is best to sand to 150-grit paper by machine and then give a quick re-sand by hand with 120 grit to straighten out any swirl marks.

Steaming Dents

Dents can be steamed out using water and a hot iron. The moisture and heat help to swell the damaged wood fibers. (1) I purposely hit this piece of poplar with a hammer to put a nice dent in it to illustrate how you can steam out a dent in a piece of wood. (2) Put a few drops of water right in the dent. (3) Then, using a hot iron, steam the dent out. I steamed out this dent using the iron raised about $\frac{1}{16}''$ above the surface of the wood. You can also use an iron with a damp rag placed over the dent. The trick to this is to check the progress of raising the dent often and not to burn the wood. (4) The dent is gone! Now with light sanding, no one will ever know this piece was damaged at all.

Dents

Wet the Dent

Apply Heat

The Raised Dent

STEP 8

Scrape off any excess glue. Dried glue will usually chip right off. Make sure your scraper has a good, sharp edge. The secret is to not have *any* excess glue, but it is inevitable. When gluing up pieces keep a clean, very damp rag handy and immediately wipe off glue that squeezes out. All the excess glue must be wiped off. If you just smear it around, all you're doing is making a bigger spot that soaks even more into the grain. Another alternative is to not touch the glue until it dries, and then chip it off.

STEP 9

Any loose veneer needs to be glued down. Use slightly thinned carpenter's glue in a syringe and carefully insert the needle under the loose spot. Cover the area with wax paper and clamp. If the spot is in an area that can't easily be clamped, put a heavy weight on it or carefully apply pressure with a hot iron. Hold down loose veneer on edges with masking tape.

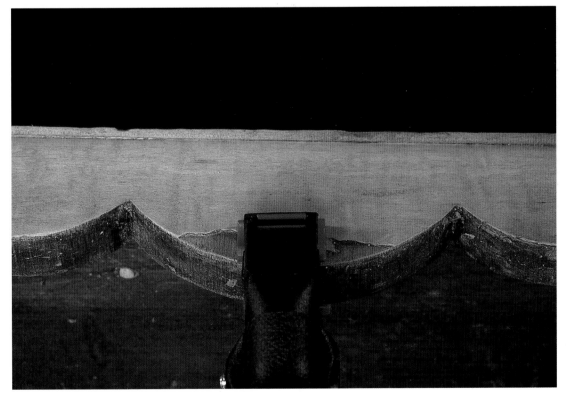

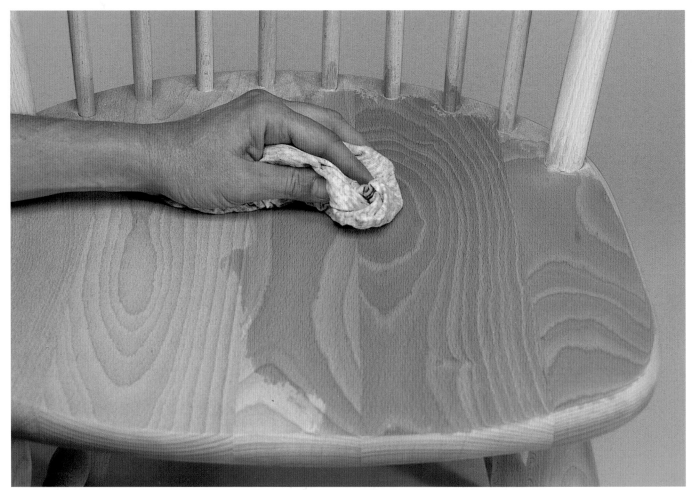

STEP 10

If there's any possibility that water has gotten on the piece (this includes perspiration from all your sanding!) wet the entire piece. Wetting the piece before the final sanding is a good idea anyway. If you look carefully, you can see glue spots, and the water lifts the little fibers of wood, making them easier to sand off for a smooth surface. When using water-borne finishes, wet the wood after the 120-grit sanding and then lightly re-sand with 150 grit.

TIP

Glue pieces of hard leather or rubber to your clamps. This keeps them from digging into the wood and making dents.

Abrasives

There are three basic kinds of abrasives used in wood finishing: sandpaper, steel wool and nylon pads. All three come in different degrees of coarseness or grit, and each grit has a very specific purpose.

Sandpaper is the most complicated of the abrasives because so many different choices are available. The first choice is the type of material that is used for the abrasive. The most common are flint, garnet, aluminum oxide and silicon carbide. Aluminum oxide, usually tan colored, is the hardest and is recommended for sanding raw wood. Silicon carbide, which is grayish blue, is also very hard and is recommended for sanding finishes.

These abrasives are glued to paper that also comes in different types. They are graded by the thickness of the paper. *A-weight* is light and flexible. It is recommended for finish sanding and wet sanding because it is less likely to cut into the finish. *C-weight* is much stronger but less flexible and is used for sanding raw wood by hand or with a small portable sander. *D-weight* is the strongest and least flexible that most finishers use. It is especially good for rough sanding by hand or machine. The key to your decision on paper is that the paper should not tear up before the abrasive quality is gone. A special waterproof paper is made for wet sanding. It is almost always black or gray and is labeled *wet/dry*.

The abrasives glued to the paper come in different sizes or grits—the larger the size, the coarser the sanding scratches. Grits are organized by how many pieces of abrasive are in a square inch. So 80-grit paper is much coarser than 400 grit. A general rule of thumb is to sand raw wood to 120 grit. Start sanding finishes with 150 or 220 grit.

Steel wool also comes in a variety of grades that are determined by the thickness of the wire with higher numbers being coarser. #2 steel wool is medium coarse and handy for stripping paint or varnish. #0000 is very fine steel wool and should be used for rubbing or smoothing finishes. The use of steel wool on raw wood is not recommended because the little wires are snagged easily by the wood fibers.

For smoothing wood turnings or carvings use a nylon scrub pad. These are also excellent for smoothing the finish between coats especially when using water-based finishes. Nylon scrub pads come in different grits ranging from very coarse to ultra-fine. The coarsest is handy for stripping; fine is good for finish sanding; and ultra-fine is perfect for rubbing out a finish.

Rich Oil Finish on a Walnut Box

The first finish I ever tried was Danish Oil—and it's still one of my favorites. Beautiful woods don't need much to enhance their beauty and nothing beats the natural look and feel of an oil finish. The finishing process itself, while hard work, is very rewarding because it's simple and natural.

Danish Oil is manufactured under a variety of names by many manufacturers. Generically it is an oil (usually tung or linseed), thinned with mineral spirits and "beefed up" with a small amount of varnish.

The truest of "close to the wood" finishes, Danish Oil is absorbed into the wood itself and hardens below the surface. There is no surface film formed like there is with varnish, shellac, lacquer and other film finishes. If you scratch an oiled surface, nothing flakes off. It's only the wood. That's the beauty—and the downfall—of it.

Oil finishes don't offer a lot of protection from heat, moisture, stains or scratching. But if you put the effort into creating a piece of furniture with a beautiful, glowing oil finish, it deserves the extra care!

Although Danish Oil can be applied to any wood, it doesn't do much for woods without a lot of natural character. Pine, oak, birch and poplar look better with other types of finishes. For oil finishes, stick to the "beautiful" woods—like walnut, cherry, mahogany and birdseye maple.

You Need

- Danish Oil finish
- bucket or foil lined tray
- inexpensive natural bristle brush
- sandpaper—120, 400 wet/dry, 600 wet/dry, 1000 wet/dry
- sanding block
- cotton swabs
- cotton rags

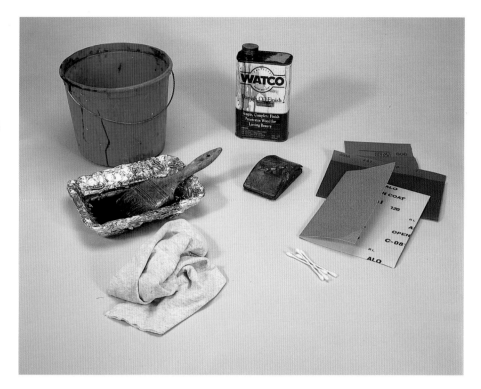

Danger! Spontaneous Combustion!

I never really believed the stories about oil rags mysteriously catching on fire until I saw it happen. Any finish that dries by oxidation generates heat during the drying process. If rags are piled on top of each other, enough heat is generated to start a fire.

Submerge all oil soaked rags in water and then lay out to dry. Do not dry them in a clothes drier, as this also runs the risk of igniting the oils that are still in the rags. Let the rags dry thoroughly, then throw away.

This box is made from solid walnut and walnut-veneered plywood. A rubbed in Danish Oil finish makes it glow. This finish was chosen for this first project because it is the least complicated of any finish.

Step-by-Step Directions

STEP 1
Preparation (10 minutes)

Check carefully for any joints or dents that need to be filled. Depending on the complexity of the piece you're working on, it may be easier to disassemble it before proceeding. With a folded quarter sheet of 120 grit sand the inside edges of the frame on the top of the box. Slightly round off sharp edges. When sanding the molding at the ends of the box, be extra careful not to get cross-grain scratches on the flat surface.

STEP 2
Detail Sanding (15 minutes)

Since this is a small surface, there is no need to use a sanding block. Use the strength of the folded sandpaper to help get into corners. Always sand in the direction of the grain—it's a little difficult in corners like this, but cross-grain scratches will really show up.

STEP 3
Taping Miters
When sanding into a miter joint (the 45° angles on the top of the box where the frame pieces meet), it sometimes helps to place a piece of masking tape over the edge of the joint. Run your sandpaper right over the tape. Then re-mask to sand the other piece.

STEP 4
Sanding Miters
Once you get comfortable sanding into miters, there's no need to tape. Simply place the sandpaper at the same angle as the miter joint. This lets you reach all the way into the joint without over sanding the narrow part.

STEP 5
Apply the Oil (5 minutes)

Pour the oil into a foil lined tray or bucket. Fully load an inexpensive, natural bristle brush and apply the oil. Don't worry about brushstrokes or direction. All you're trying to do is get a wet, fairly even application of oil on as quickly as possible. Make sure the entire surface is covered—especially edges and corners—but don't let it pool up there. It will just make extra work for you later.

STEP 6
Coat the Entire Piece

On a small project like this, go ahead and coat out the entire piece. On larger projects it's more practical to work on one surface at a time.

STEP 7
Let the Oil Soak In (10 minutes)

After the oil has soaked in for about ten minutes, check for any areas that have totally absorbed all the oil. They will appear dry and dull. Apply more oil to those surfaces.

STEP 8
Sand in the Oil (15 minutes)

Then take a quarter sheet of wet/dry 400-grit sandpaper and wrap it around a rubber sanding block. Dip the paper in the oil and start sanding. Then keep sanding. Pretty soon the oil will start getting thicker and there will be a lot of resistance to the sanding block. Now you can stop sanding.

TIP
Both sides of any surface should receive equal amounts of finish. This helps keep the wood stable and prevents moisture from being absorbed.

STEP 9
Wipe off the Excess Oil (3 minutes)

Wipe any excess oil off with a soft cotton rag. Get it as clean as you can. Turn your cloth frequently and keep wiping until no more oil comes off. Immediately place all rags in a bucket of water.

STEP 10
Clean out the Corners (3 minutes)

Use a cotton swab to clean out corners or carvings. There should be no oil sitting on the surface of the wood. Once you're done, set the piece aside for at least a couple hours. After about an hour, make sure no oil is "leeching" out of the pores or corners (it will look shiny compared to the satiny sheen of the rest of the piece). If there is, wipe it off with a rag.

STEP 11
Apply Several Coats of Oil (20 minutes)

Apply a second coat of oil using the same technique as before. This time, really work the oil into the grain of the wood. This is one of the few times you have official permission to go against the grain of the wood.

STEP 12
Sanding Into Corners

Sand the oil in as before, but use 600-grit paper. To get into corners, use a quarter sheet of paper folded in fourths. Follow the same wiping procedure.

STEP 13

Use Sanding Block on Flat Surface
After the piece sits for at least a couple of hours, repeat the process with 600-grit paper. Remember to use a block on flat surfaces. For an extra nice finish, end up with 1000-grit paper.

Maintaining the Finish

An oil finish definitely takes some maintenance. There is no one schedule that applies universally. Depending on the usage and where the piece is located, it may need to be re-oiled anywhere from every six months to once a year. There are special "maintenance oils" or you can just repeat the final oiling step. If an area has been damaged, rub the spot with #0000 steel wool, sand in a coat with 800 grit, then do the entire surface with 1000 grit.

Variations

If you want the beautiful depth of an oil finish but need more maintenance-free protection, apply a topcoat of lacquer or varnish to your project. It is very important to let the oil cure thoroughly before top-coating. Seventy-two hours is recommended—I would give it a couple more days than that.

CHAPTER 2

Easy Gel Stain and Varnish Finish on an Oak Shelf

Gel stains are an excellent product for anyone who is new to wood finishing. They are the most consistent stain available and very easy to use. Because they are so thick, gel stains don't flow on their own—they only go where you put them. This has two advantages. The first is that the stain won't run or drip onto surfaces where you don't want it. It makes the application take a little longer, but saves a lot of time cleaning up and fixing mistakes.

The second and more important advantage is that the stain stays mainly on the surface of the wood as opposed to the more liquid stains and dyes that really soak in. This is crucial on woods like pine and birch that absorb stains very unevenly and can easily look splotchy after staining. Gel stains almost guarantee a splotch-free finish if proper preparation has been done.

This lack of penetration is also the drawback of gel stains. Gel stains produce a flatter overall color compared to liquid stains and dyes whose deeper penetration really "pops" the grain and beauty of the wood. So for the "beautiful" woods like mahogany, walnut and exotic veneers, gel stains are not the best choice.

The finish used on this project is also an excellent choice for beginning finishers. Oil-based varnishes are easy to brush on and re-coat, don't require a lot of fancy equipment, and provide a durable, beautiful finish.

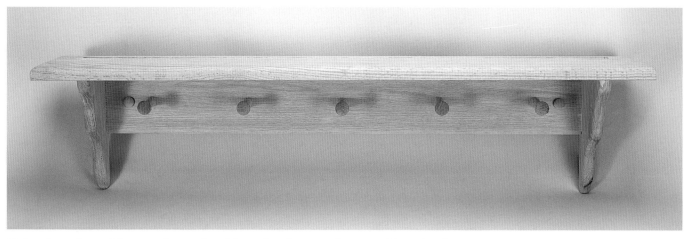

Gel stain and varnish were chosen for this project because they provide a simple way to finish this solid oak shelf coat rack. This is a very good project for people new to finishing.

You Need

- gel stain
- oil-based varnish
- natural bristle stain brush
- natural bristle varnish brush
- sandpaper—120-grit aluminum oxide and 220-grit silicon carbide
- tack rag
- stir stick
- cotton rag

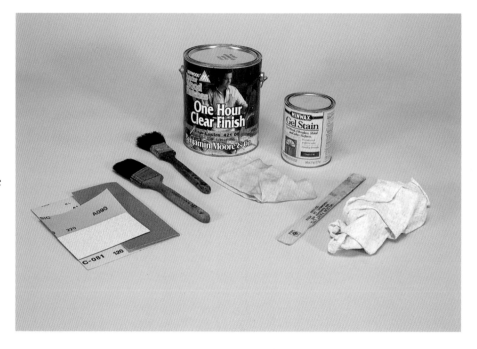

KEYS TO SUCCESS

- If you use a power sander, remove any of the sanding marks before you stain. Even though gel stain doesn't penetrate deeply, these will still show up as darker scratches on your finished project.

- Always test your stain on a sample board or an area of the piece that won't show. Check for color and pay attention to how long you leave the stain on. The longer a stain sits on a piece, the darker the color will be.

- Try to varnish in a dust-free environment. This is a finisher's fantasy, but take all the precautions you can. Don't wear clothes that shed a lot of lint and don't let your pet anywhere near a wet piece!

Step-by-Step Directions

STEP 1
Preparation (15 minutes)

This piece would have been a lot easier to sand and finish if the pegs hadn't been glued in by the manufacturer. Sand as carefully as possible around them. Because the gel stain is so thick, you might have to work your staining brush back and forth in the groove to ensure 100 percent coverage.

STEP 2
Apply Stain (10 minutes)

Brush on a generous coat of stain on the entire piece. Large pieces may have to be divided into sections to prevent the stain from drying up.

STEP 3
Wipe off Stain (10 minutes)

After the stain sits for about five minutes, wipe it clean with a soft cotton rag. Be sure to get all the excess stain out of the grooves and corners.

STEP 4
Wipe Clean for High Contrast

The cleaner the stain is wiped off, the greater the contrast will be between the grain and the wood.

STEP 5
Apply First Coat of Varnish
(15 minutes)

Before you begin varnishing, develop a plan of attack so you can coat all the surfaces without having to handle wet areas. One way to approach this is to partially drive four nails into the back. Varnish the back first and flip the piece on to the nails. This gives access to all sides and keeps wet varnish edges off the table. Next, varnish the inside area where the pegs are. Grab the rack by the outside and turn it around to make it easier to varnish the top.

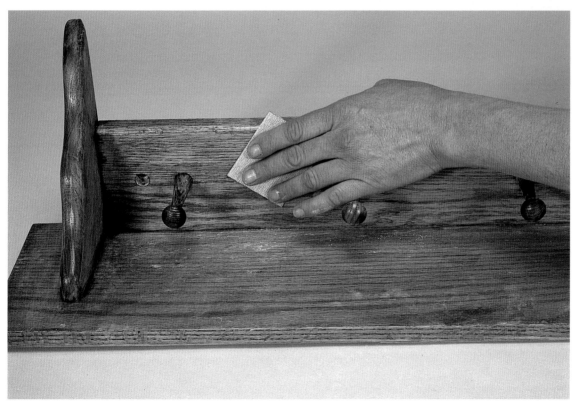

STEP 6
Sand Varnish (5 minutes)

Let the varnish dry at least three hours. Some varnishes require a much longer drying time. Check the manufacturer's directions for re-coat time. To tell if a finish is dry enough to sand and re-coat, lightly press your fingernail into the finish. It should not leave an impression. Use a quarter sheet of 220-grit sandpaper folded in fourths to get into these small areas. Corners will need special attention because that is where dust tends to accumulate and it's harder to smoothly brush out the finish.

TIP
Never shake varnish because air bubbles may get trapped in the finish and transferred to your project. It is important to thoroughly stir all products because some components of finishes and stains settle out rather quickly.

STEP 7
Apply Second Coat of Varnish (15 minutes)

My favorite brush for varnishing is a natural bristle sash brush that is cut at an angle on the end. This makes it easier to get into corners and around the pegs. Dip the bristles about one third of the way into the varnish and press them against the side of the can to remove excess material. Brush the length of the corner and then place the bristle tips right into the corner and gently pull the finish out in the direction of the grain of the wood.

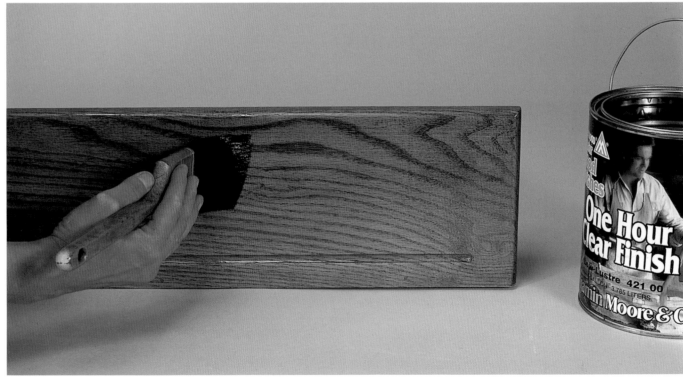

STEP 8
Follow the Grain

Hold the brush between your thumb and forefinger with your other fingers resting on the ferrule—the metal piece that holds in the bristles. Press the brush firmly enough to bend the bristles about one third of their length. Always brush in the direction of the grain. That way any brushstrokes that don't flow out will be disguised by the grain pattern.

STEP 9
Finish Coats (20 minutes)

Apply one or two more coats of finish. Remove all sanding dust with a tack rag before re-coating. An easy way to do narrow edges is to first lightly tap the brush along the whole length. Then do a light stroke with a fairly dry brush the whole length in the direction of the grain. If dust gets in the finish as it is drying, let the finish cure for a couple days and then rub with #0000 steel wool and some polish.

Caring for Brushes

A good quality, natural bristle brush will last for years if properly taken care of. Brushes should be cleaned immediately after use to prevent stain or finish from drying in them.

First rinse the brush in the appropriate solvent—mineral spirits for oil base, alcohol for shellac, and water for latex and other water-based products. Most manufacturers provide information on the can for clean up if you are not sure which solvent to use.

Dip the brush all the way into the solvent and swish it around. Then hold the brush upside down and squeeze the bristles to force the solvent out at the base of the brush. This will flush out any remaining material that might be pooled in the ferrule. Repeat this process until the brush is clean. You might have to change the solvent a couple times. Wear gloves to do this.

Some people like to store their brushes suspended by hooks in clean solvent. I prefer to store mine dry. I take the cleaning one step further and wash the brushes in warm soapy water. After an initial rinsing, spin the brush between the palms of your hands to force all material to the tips of the brush. Rinse again, spin one more time, carefully re-shape the brush and hang to dry.

Maintaining the Finish

The need for frequent furniture polishing is a greatly overrated myth. Most finishes, including this varnish finish, need to be dusted once a week with a feather duster or treated dust cloth. Polishing once a month with a good, non-oily furniture polish is plenty. More polishing just builds up a layer of oil that actually attracts more dust. Once or twice a year, a heavily used piece may need to be washed with a mild solution of soap and water. Wring your rag out well and don't get the furniture very wet. Dry immediately with a soft cotton cloth.

Variations

There are many types of stain that can be used right from the can. Pigmented wiping stains are also easy to use. The main difference between wiping stains and gel stains is that wiping stains are much thinner and absorb more into the wood. The downside of this is that some woods—like birch and pine—may look splotchy. The upside is that the stain wipes off cleanly and gives a less opaque look.

Step-by-Step Directions

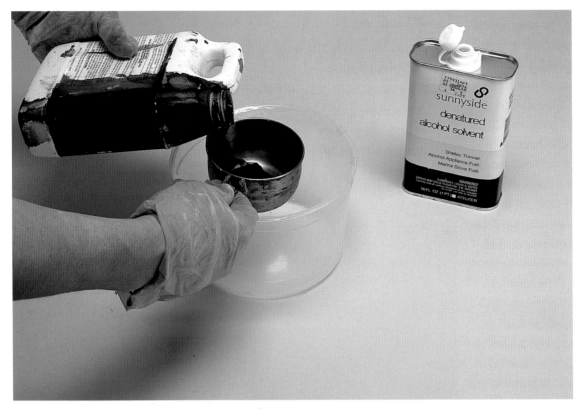

STEP 1
Preparation (30 minutes)

Sand thoroughly through 120 grit. Take care when sanding into the joint of the apron and the leg—use a smaller piece of folded sandpaper and sand with the grain right into the joint. Mix an eighth cup of brown aniline dye with one quart of denatured alcohol.

STEP 2
Dyeing the Wood (20 minutes)

To get really deep penetration of the dye, apply a wet coat of dye using a sponge applicator. The darkness of the dye is controlled more by its concentration than by the amount applied. It is easier to work on a piece like this if you remove the top from the base.

STEP 3
Dealing With Drips (5 minutes)

It is a good practice to dye from the bottom up because the initial application is what will show. A drip onto an already wet surface won't show, but it will if it's on a dry surface. Notice how the dye dropped over the edge on this board.

STEP 4
Repair the Mistake (5 minutes)

Since I forgot to dye the edges of the table top first and got a run onto an edge, I had to re-sand the entire edge with 120 grit and re-dye it.

STEP 5
Let the Dye Dry (10 minutes)

When the aniline dye dries it will have an even, flat appearance with no darker wet spots. This usually takes about ten minutes—more if you applied a really wet application or if there is very high humidity. If water is used to dilute the aniline instead of alcohol, lightly sand the surface to cut down raised fibers. On some woods a wet application of alcohol-based dye will also significantly raise the grain and should also be sanded. This photo shows the table top as the dye is drying. Notice how the dry area on the right is much lighter than the area that is still wet.

STEP 6
Apply the Sealer Coat (20 minutes)

This brand of polyurethane (sold nationally under the Graham label) recommends using a thinned application for the sealer coat. Some brands suggest a separate sealer and others recommend using a full-strength coat for the first application. Follow the directions on the can—manufacturers do a lot of research on their product and know what works best. I thinned this polyurethane with 15 percent mineral spirits for the first coat.

Apply a wet coat of the thinned polyurethane. Notice how the depth of color returns with the application of finish. With a fully loaded brush, begin your stroke a couple inches from the edge of the table and pull it completely off the other side.

STEP 7
Overlap Your Strokes

Repeat the process from the other way, overlapping your first stroke. Never begin your stroke with the bristles over the edge or the finish will be raked out of your brush and cause a drip. When finishing the legs, apply finish to the insides of the legs first so you're not reaching past freshly coated surfaces. Don't forget to seal the bottoms of the legs. This will help protect the wood from moisture soaking up through the end grain of the feet.

STEP 8
Varnishing Into a Corner (1 minute)

To varnish into a corner, first coat the corner then place the tip of the brush near the corner and pull away from it. This technique ensures good coverage in the corners while it prevents too much buildup that could run or look sloppy.

STEP 9
Varnishing Away From a Corner
Brush the varnish to the middle of this table apron. Then coat out the opposite corner pulling your brushstrokes all the way into the wet varnish on the other side. Pull the brush away lightly as you overlap into the wet varnish.

STEP 10
Sand the Sealer Coat (20 minutes)
Follow the manufacturer's recommendations for re-coat time. These vary greatly from brand to brand. Don't try to re-coat sooner than suggested—the finish may feel dry, but not be properly cured. Sand lightly with 220-grit stearated paper.

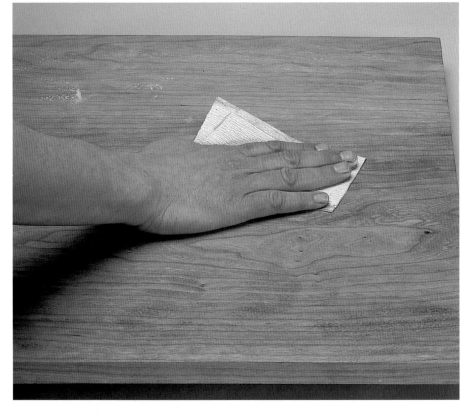

TIP
As you are brushing on a finish try to have a light shining to the side so when you look across the surface you can immediately see if you skipped any areas. If caught right away, these areas can be brushed out.

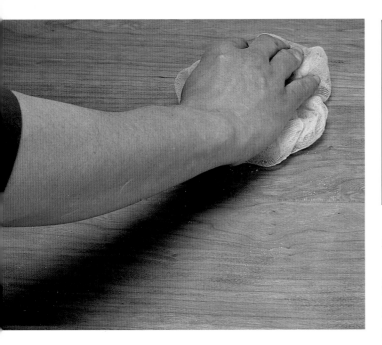

TIP

Even though varnish and polyurethane take hours to dry to the touch, they do start to set up within minutes. Once this happens, the finish starts to feel like honey and should be left alone. Going back to it at this point will only leave brush marks and create a worse problem for you to fix later.

STEP 11
Tack off the Sanding Dust (2 minutes)

Remove the white sanding dust with a tack cloth. The stearated paper causes the finish to really powder when it's sanded. This is good because it prevents the paper from gumming up and scratching the finish. But all of the sanding dust needs to be removed or it will get trapped in the next layer of finish causing bumps or a light haze.

STEP 12
Apply the Final Coats (40 minutes)

Strain the varnish into a clean container. It's always a good idea to strain the finish even if it's a brand new can.

STEP 13
Loading the Brush

Dip your natural bristle brush about one third of the way into the varnish and then lightly flex it against the side of the container to remove the excess. Resist the urge to drag the brush across the lip of the container as this will remove too much material and fill the polyurethane with air bubbles that will be transferred to your piece.

STEP 14
Topping Off (20 minutes)

After a number of strokes, go back to the beginning and lightly re-brush the polyurethane. On a small top like this, go ahead and brush on the initial application over the entire surface. You will have to divide larger surfaces into sections. The key is to re-brush the polyurethane before it starts to set up. If your brush feels like it is dragging instead of gliding, you have waited too long. Without adding any more polyurethane, hold the brush at a right angle so only the tips of the bristles touch. With a light touch, repeat the brushstrokes of the initial application. This smooths out the finish, removes air bubbles, and fills in any areas that might have been skipped.

STEP 15
Finishing the Edges (5 minutes)

Edges and narrow surfaces require special brushing techniques. When the brush is much wider than the surface being coated, the bristles will splay out and apply an uneven coat. On this table edge, first apply the polyurethane across the grain in an up and down motion. Then lightly pull the brush sideways, following the grain for a smooth finish.

Removing Bristles From Wet Finish

It seems that no matter how expensive the brush, some bristles fall out—inevitably on your final coat of finish. If you notice it before the finish starts to set up, delicately scoop the loose bristle up with the tip of the brush and grab it with your free hand. A thin needle or pin also works well. Gently overbrush the area to smooth out the indentation left by the bristle. If the finish has already started to set, leave the bristle alone until the finish is dry. Then take a straightedged razor blade and drag it over the bristle. It should pop it loose. Sand and re-coat the surface.

STEP 16
Finish the Project (1 hour)

⬤ After an overnight dry, sand the table to remove surface defects and brush marks. Apply another coat of polyurethane. Let dry at least 48 hours and then wet sand with 400-grit paper. Follow with #0000 steel wool and polish or wax.

Variations

Polyurethane can easily be sprayed with both conventional and HVLP (high-volume, low-pressure) systems. Because it dries so much slower than lacquer, take care not to get runs. Spray on thin coats and let dry thoroughly between coats.

The same look can be achieved with a totally water-based finish system. A small amount of aniline dye added to the water-based finish will duplicate the amberness and warmth of polyurethane.

Warm Glaze and Shellac Finish on a Walnut Picture Frame

On this project, we'll take a beautiful wood, walnut, and enhance its beauty by imitating the patina that develops with time. Patina is the glow and depth of color that comes from years of exposure to light, use and the elements. New walnut looks grayish and cold but develops a golden glow with darker overtones over the years. The golden glow and darker recesses can't be accomplished in one step, so we used a combination of dyes and glazes to speed the passage of time.

For the protective finish on this project we'll use a spray can of shellac. Shellac is one of the oldest finishes used and is made from the secretions of the lac bug. It is dissolved in alcohol and can be bought pre-mixed for brushing or spraying, in flake form or in spray cans. It is quick drying and a little tricky to brush, so a spray can application is easier for a novice finisher.

You Need

- sandpaper—120-grit aluminum oxide, 400-grit stearated
- red and yellow aniline dye
- spray can of shellac
- Guardsman Warm Brown Glaze
- gloves
- sponge brush
- natural bristle brush
- cotton rag
- measuring spoons
- tack rag

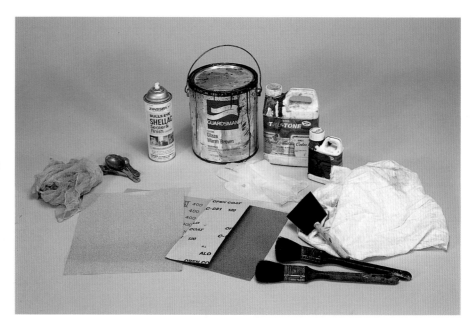

KEYS TO SUCCESS

❧ Spray multiple thin coats rather than a few heavy coats to prevent sags and runs.

❧ Do a sample on a scrap piece of wood to check the strength of the dye before applying it to the piece. The dye looks very different when it is dry than when a finish coat is put on.

❧ Remove all sanding dust before applying dye or stain. Do not use a tack cloth on raw wood—it can leave a residue on the surface. Instead, use a vacuum cleaner or old brush.

With a few simple steps, a new walnut frame takes on the appearance of beautifully aged wood. This finish is especially effective on carved pieces because it really highlights the carving and imitates the natural aging and coloring of wood that has been waxed for many years.

Step-by-Step Directions

STEP 1
Scrape off Dry Glue (5 minutes)

Check for any glue that might have squeezed through at the joints. Take a sharp chisel and carefully pry off the dried glue.

Removing Glue From Joints

Any glue that sits on the wood surface will prevent stain from absorbing and will show up as a light spot. The best solution to glue spotting is prevention. Don't use any more glue than is needed—only a tiny bead should squeeze out when you clamp a joint. There are two ways to deal with the glue that squeezes out. The first is to wipe it with a wet rag. If you do this, make sure your rag is wet enough to remove all the glue and not just spread it around. If you use this approach, wet down the entire piece so you don't get a water spot. The other approach is to let the glue dry and chip it off with a sharp chisel or razor blade.

STEP 2
Sand Inside the Frame
(10 minutes)

Sand the frame with 120-grit sandpaper. A quarter sheet of sandpaper folded in fourths will roll into a shape that easily sands the curved surfaces of the frame. Sand all the way into the corner.

STEP 3
Sand the Outside Contours
(10 minutes)

Fold the paper to a shape that matches the contours of the *outside* of the frame.

STEP 4
Wet Down the Frame (2 minutes)
With a sponge brush go over the frame with water to ensure even absorbtion of the dye.

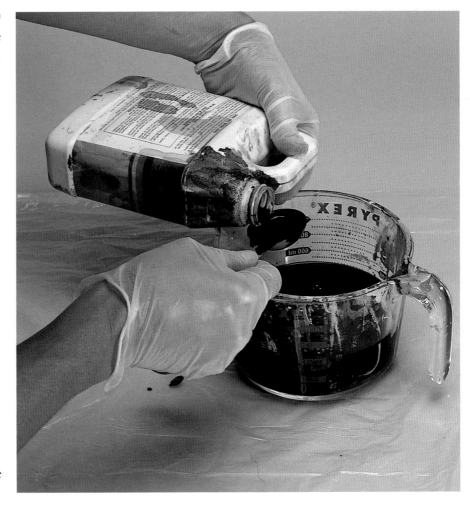

STEP 5
Mix the Dye (10 minutes)
Mix two tablespoons of red and two tablespoons of yellow aniline dye in one quart of warm water.

STEP 6
Apply a Coat of Dye (10 minutes)

Use the same brush to apply a wet coat of dye. If excess dye pools up in the grooves, soak it up with the tip of the sponge brush.

STEP 7
Let the Dye Dry (1 hour)

Let the dye thoroughly dry. As it dries the wood will begin to look much lighter and "dustier"—this is normal. The color of the dyed wood will return once finish is applied.

STEP 8
Apply the First Coat of Shellac (2 minutes)

Shake the can of shellac for a minute. Spraying out of a can is really no different than using a spray gun—instead of pulling a trigger, you push the button. Begin spraying a couple inches away from the piece and put on a thin, wet coat. Notice the change in color once the shellac hits the dye. Continue spraying a couple inches past the piece. Overlap the strokes to ensure total coverage.

STEP 9
Sand the Finish (5 minutes)

After the shellac has dried (about 20 minutes), sand with 400-grit stearated paper. All you are trying to do is smooth the surface of defects, so use a light touch. Run your hand over the surface to make sure you have gotten rid of any bumps. Pay special attention to the corner joints.

STEP 10
Tack off the Dust (2 minutes)

The sanding dust will have a slightly white appearance—wipe all this off with a tack cloth.

TIP

All the same technique and safety precautions should be followed using a spray can as spraying with a spray gun. Make sure you have plenty of ventilation. Keep the spray can about 12 inches away from the surface you are spraying. Use consistent, overlapping strokes. Start each stroke a couple inches from the edge of the piece and keep spraying a couple inches over—this prevents buildup on the edges.

STEP 11
Glaze the Frame (2 minutes)

Dip about one inch of a natural bristle brush into the glaze and brush onto the wood. The application of the glaze does not have to be especially neat—just get it on as evenly as possible.

STEP 12
Wipe the Glaze (5 minutes)

Remove the excess glaze with a soft cotton rag. The rag should be small enough to fit comfortably in your hand without "tails" hanging off. Wipe harder on the high surfaces and leave more glaze down in the grooves.

Tack Rags

Tack rags are used to pick up loose pieces of dust and other material between coats of finish. Wiping with a plain rag, brushing with a dry brush, or blowing off with compressed air will only put the material in the air and it will inevitably fall on a freshly coated finish. A vacuum cleaner with a brush attachment works great for picking up sanding dust. But a vacuum can be dangerous when used to pick up finish sanding residue—especially from lacquer—because it creates static electricity that could cause a spark.

Many people advocate making their own tack rags. If you really want to do it, take some cheesecloth or a cotton rag and lightly wet with a thinned mix of the finish you are using.

But why bother? Tack rags are not that expensive and last quite a long time. One rag should get you through the entire finishing process on a piece of furniture. And manufacturers have spent a lot of time and money figuring out what just the right amount of tack is. Too much tack and the rag will stick to the surface and mar it—too little, and it doesn't do any good.

Tack rags are usually packaged in individual plastic wrappers. Remove the rag and completely unfold it. Lightly crumple it into a ball and quickly wipe the surface. Needless to say, the finish must be completely dry. Also use extra caution on hot, sunny days if you are finishing outside. The heat makes the finish more susceptible to marring from the rag. Use very light strokes and don't let the rag sit still on the surface. As the rag becomes full, shake it out and reform the loose ball so that a clean area is touching the wood surface. When you are through tacking off the surface, place the rag in a reclosable plastic bag to keep it from drying out.

CHAPTER 5

Professional Filled and Dyed Finish on a Mahogany and Sapele Briefcase

This project combines a number of steps covered in previous projects and adds the step of filling the wood pore. It shows how different procedures can be combined on a project. Even though the final finish is a sprayed pre-catalyzed lacquer, you can do all the steps leading up to it and brush on your finish of choice.

Pre-catalyzed lacquer is a fairly new kind of finish combining the beauty of a lacquer finish with the durability of modern catalyzed finishes. It involves a chemical reaction in the finish that causes it to dry to a harder, more durable film. Most catalyzed lacquers are also higher in solids—the material that's left after the finish dries—and so require

fewer coats to build up the finish. Only 3 to 4 coats are usually needed compared to the 10 to 20 coats traditional nitrocellulose lacquer requires.

Pre-catalyzed lacquer must be sprayed because it dries so quickly. It contains dangerous solvents and strict safety precautions must be followed.

You Need

- sandpaper—120-grit aluminum oxide, 220- and 400-grit silicon carbide, 400- and 1000-grit wet/dry
- red and brown aniline dye
- Guardsman dark walnut wood filler
- Guardsman Warm Brown Glaze
- burlap
- cotton rags
- natural bristle brushes (one stiff and one soft)
- quart spray gun
- compressor (not in photo)
- respirator with organic vapor cartridges
- ventilation system (not in photo)
- tack cloth
- stir stick
- #0000 steel wool
- measuring spoons and cup
- Mohawk wool lube
- denatured alcohol
- M.L. Campbell Magnalac pre-catalyzed lacquer
- wooden toothpicks
- sanding block

KEYS TO SUCCESS

- Allow plenty of drying time between steps. Even though the filler and glaze may look and feel dry, it's important that all the solvents evaporate before a coat of finish is applied. Rushing the process may cause cloudiness or even finish failure.

- Don't try to fill a large surface by yourself because the filler will get hard and become almost impossible to remove. Have someone help you or divide the surface into workable sections.

- Always remember that a finish is only as good as the preparation you do. Sanding may not be fun, but it is the most important step in the finishing process.

The natural beauty of mahogany and sapele are emphasized by a furniture-type finish. A small project like this is a good way to try out some techniques used in creating a high-end furniture finish. The characteristics of this finish are a clarity of color that enhances rather than masks the beauty of the wood and a totally filled grain that gives the piece a silky smooth feel.

Step-by-Step Directions

STEP 1
Preparation (45 minutes)

Disassemble the briefcase and re-move the maple inserts. If the project you're finishing has a part that is not going to be stained but can't be removed, carefully mask it off after it has been sanded to 120 grit. Use a high quality brown masking tape that doesn't leave adhesive residue when removed. Burnish all edges of the tape with your fingernail to keep stain from soaking through. Sand all parts with 120-grit sandpaper and prepare as needed, fol-lowing directions in the chapter on preparation. Carefully tape off the grooves where the maple inserts go so that finish doesn't get built up in them.

STEP 2
Mix the Dye (2 minutes)

Mix two table-spoons of red aniline, two table-spoons of brown ani-line and four cups of denatured alcohol.

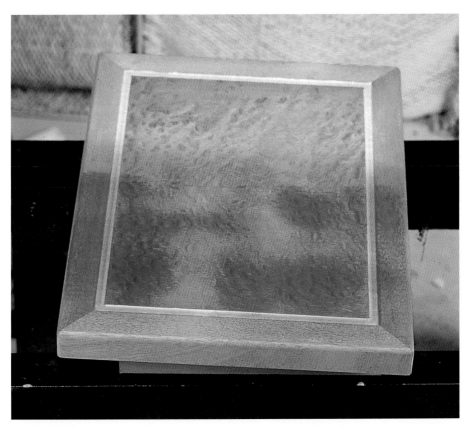

STEP 3
Spray the Dye (15 minutes)

Spray on an even coat of dye (see chapter four for spray techniques). Let dye dry. This only takes a couple minutes.

STEP 4
Don't Panic!
The dye will dry to a very different color.

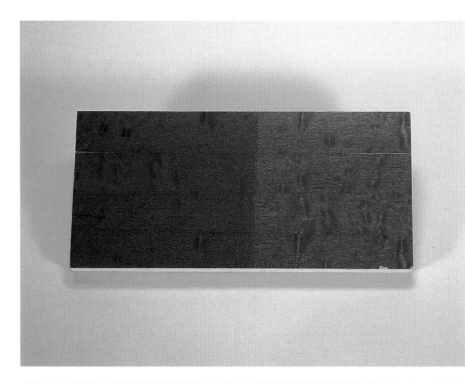

STEP 4A
Dyed vs. Undyed
Notice the difference in color from the dyed sapele on the left to the undyed sapele on the right.

STEP 5
Apply the Filler (10 minutes)
Apply the filler with a short napped, natural bristle brush. Guardsman's filler is formulated to be used as it comes in the can but some manufacturers recommend thinning theirs.

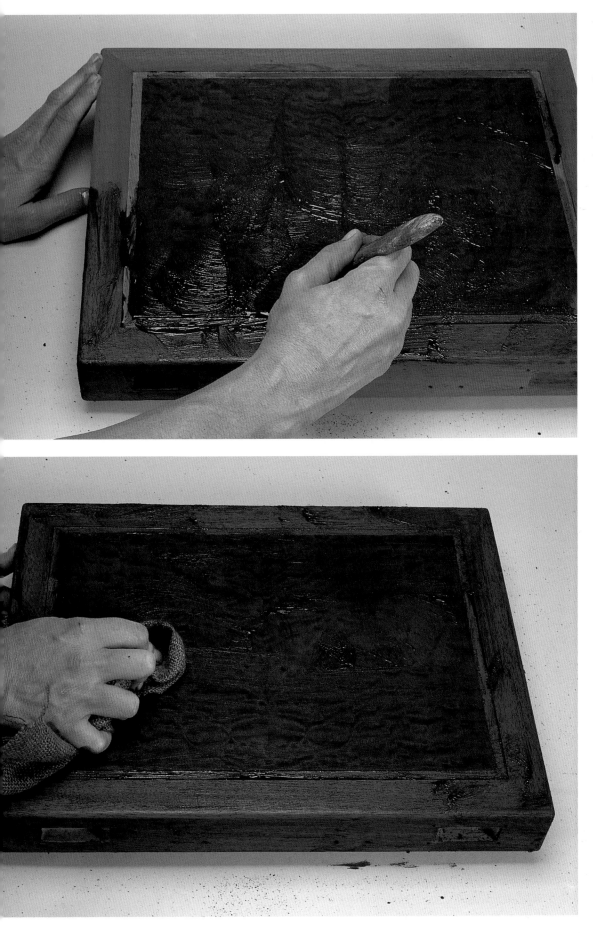

STEP 6
Work Filler In
(5 minutes)
Work the filler in with the brush in a circular motion, making sure you get 100 percent wet coverage.

STEP 7
Rub in the Filler With Burlap
(15 minutes)
Rub the filler into the grain using a burlap rag and a cross-grained motion. On the narrow edges, use a circular motion to work the filler into the grain. Try to push the filler into the grain rather than wiping it off the surface.

STEP 8
Finish up With the Grain

As the filler dries and takes on a hazy, gray appearance, switch to a diagonal motion, using a little less pressure. Finish up with light pressure, going with the grain.

STEP 9
Clean out the Excess Filler (5 minutes)

Clean out corners and grooves with a sharpened wooden dowel or toothpick. Then wipe off any remaining filler with a soft cotton rag.

STEP 10
Wipe off All Residue

It is very important to get all excess filler off. If left on surface or in corners, it will dry rock hard and have an unpleasant gray appearance under the finish. Let the filler dry at least overnight.

Filler

All woods have pores. Some, like cherry and maple, have very small pores. Others, like walnut and mahogany, have medium sized pores. Woods like oak and ash have very large pores. If you run your fingernail across cherry, you will barely get any resistance—walnut will feel slightly textured and oak will definitely grab your nail.

To fill or not to fill is an aesthetic decision. Some people prefer the more natural look of unfilled wood. To others, the only truly finished wood is a totally filled finish.

Oil-based wood filler is a mixture of silica, linseed oil, pigment and mineral spirits. There are also waterborne fillers now available. Some fillers come ready to use (RTU); others must be thinned. The consistency depends on the amount of filling needed. A typical filler is about the consistency of thick pea soup.

Fillers can be bought already tinted or can be tinted with universal colorants like Cal-tints or Mixol.

Really deep pore woods, like oak or ash may require more than one application of filler. Let the first coat dry thoroughly and thin the second a little more.

This board shows the different looks created from different colors of filler. Filler is traditionally colored to a slightly darker tint than the natural wood pore. Interesting "decorator" looks can be created by tinting the filler to a lighter color.

STEP 11
Spray on the First Coat (10 minutes)

Before proceeding, smell the filler to make sure all solvents have evaporated. Lightly sand with 400-grit sandpaper to remove any remaining filler on the surface. Spray on a coat of pre-catalyzed lacquer and let dry.

TIP
Resist the urge to put on more and more coats of finish. Most finishes should not be more than 3 mils thick—about the thickness of this paper. If a catalyzed lacquer gets applied too thickly, it will start pulling against itself and crack.

STEP 12
Sand the First Coat (5 minutes)

Sand the finish with 220-grit sandpaper using a fairly light touch. Sanding will create a white powder—wipe this off with a tack rag.

STEP 13
Glaze the Mahogany (5 minutes)

Because the solid mahogany edges look flat and lifeless next to the sapele, I decided to glaze them to add more depth. Use a rag to apply a wet coat of warm brown glaze to the mahogany edges.

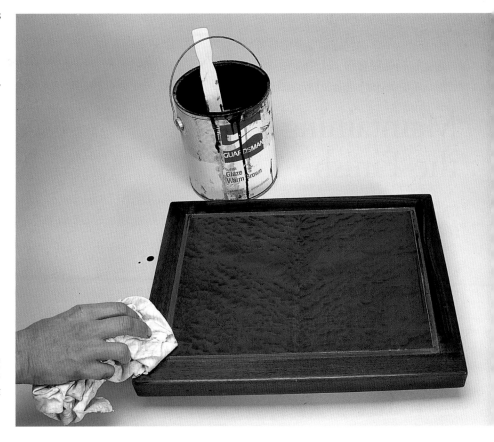

STEP 14
Wipe the Glaze (10 minutes)

Wipe the mahogany fairly clean, but do not scrub all the glaze off. Leave a transluscent layer of color. Let the glaze dry overnight and then glue in the maple inserts.

You Need

- sandpaper—120-grit aluminum oxide, 400-grit silicon carbide
- medium and fine grit Scotchbrite pads
- water-based stain
- foam applicator
- nylon bristle brush
- water-based glaze medium
- black latex paint
- rags
- tack rags
- satin Varathane water-based finish
- Famowood putty
- gloves, putty knife, stir stick
- #0000 steel wool

This project gives step-by-step directions for applying a water-based finish on a beech chair. These directions will guide you through the new world of water-based finishes that are safer to use and better for the environment.

KEYS TO SUCCESS

- Because water-based finishes work so differently than other finishes, take the time to read all the information supplied by the manufacturer. Pay special attention to drying and re-coat times.

- When buying unfinished furniture, look at the character of the wood used by the manufacturer. Try to find a piece that doesn't have a big variance in wood color.

- Just because natural bristle brushes are more expensive, doesn't mean they're the best for every job. Water-based finishes call for the use of nylon or polyester bristle brushes.

Step-by-Step Directions

STEP 1
Preparation (20 minutes)

I bought this chair from an unfinished furniture store, and it was already sanded fairly well. But a thorough sanding with 120 grit is still needed to get rid of shipping scuffs and dirt. This sanding also gives an even "openness" to the wood allowing the stain and finish to grab evenly. Follow the grain of the wood right into the spindles.

STEP 2
Putty the Nail Holes (5 minutes)

The manufacturer didn't fill any of the pin tack holes. The secret to puttying is to use as little putty as possible and keep it right where you need it. For filling small holes like this I use a "grapefruit knife" putty knife. The small, curved tip lets me get the putty right in the hole without spreading it around. The less you get on, the less you have to sand off! Sand the puttied areas with 120-grit paper. The only putty remaining should be in the nail hole. Putty left on the surrounding surface will show up as a blotch when it's stained.

 ## TIP

Use a wood putty that is a little bit lighter than the final stain color. The putty will absorb some of the stain and blend right in. If it is still too light, a little bit of color can be added using an artist's brush to apply more stain.

STEP 3
Sand the Turnings (10 minutes)

If the turnings (rungs and spindles made with a lathe) are smooth, instead of sanding with 120-grit sandpaper, use a medium grit Scotchbrite pad. Wrap the pad around the spindle and firmly rotate your hand while slowly moving down. The pad is flexible enough to get down into the nooks and crannies of the spindles.

STEP 4
Prepare the End Grain (5 minutes)

A potential problem area on this chair is the end grain around the seat. Without precautions, the end grain will suck in the stain and appear much darker than the rest of the chair. After the normal 120-grit sand, burnish the edge with a fine grit Scotchbrite. This will polish the edge and keep the stain from soaking in as much.

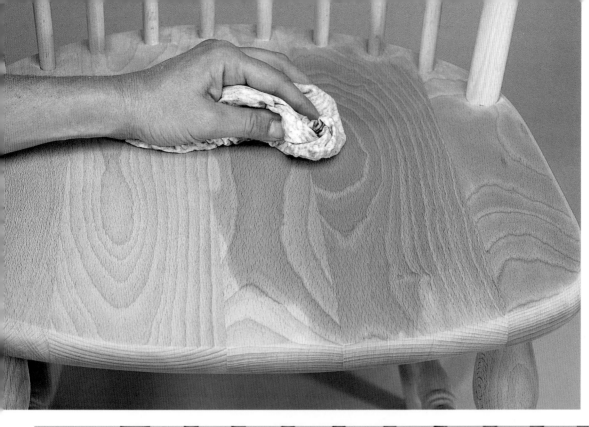

STEP 5
Raise the Grain (5 minutes)

One problem with water-based finishes is that they raise the grain of the wood. To counteract this, wet the entire chair down with a damp rag. After the wood dries, scrub it with a fine grit Scotchbrite pad. This cuts off the raised fibers and makes a surface that will absorb stain evenly.

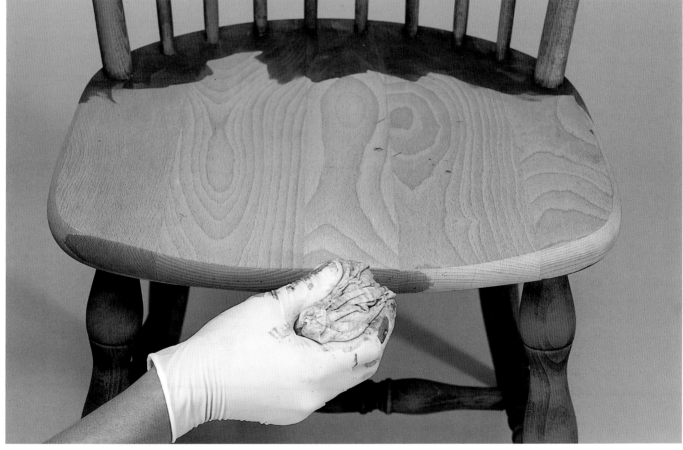

STEP 6
Apply the Stain (15 minutes)

Use a nylon brush to apply the stain to the legs and chair back. Stain one leg at a time. Make sure the stain gets all the way into the joints. Wipe with a dry rag.

Before staining the chair seat, wet the front edge with water. This is another precaution to keep the stain from soaking into the end grain—it's like saturating a sponge.

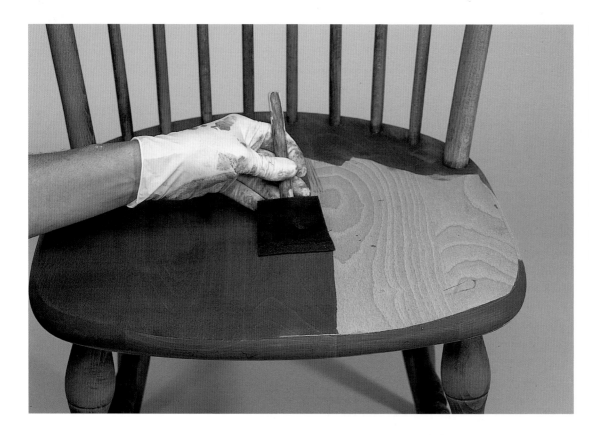

STEP 7
*Stain the Seat
(2 minutes)*

On the chair seat, it's just as fast to apply the stain with a brush. First work it around the rungs, trying not to get stain on the already stained pieces. Then quickly brush it on the rest of the rungs.

Fixing a Splotch

Because we stopped to take a picture, the stain that I got on the seat when staining the rungs dried up and left a splotch. If I had gone ahead and applied finish to this area, the splotch would have remained and looked very ugly.

To fix this, I applied extra stain to the splotchy area and worked it in with a fine Scotchbrite pad. This reactivated the stain, allowing me to wipe it clean.

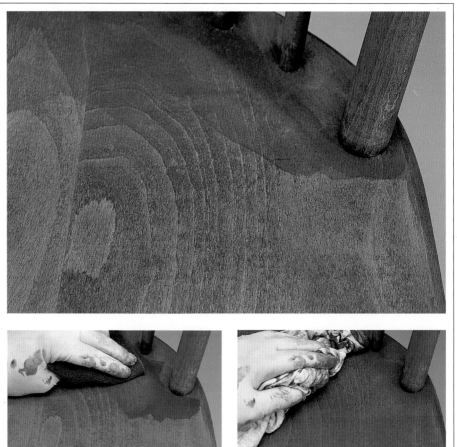

Step 1

Step 2

STEP 8
Wipe off the Stain (2 minutes)

Wipe off the excess with even strokes, following the grain pattern. Do a clean wipe, but don't scrub hard.

TIP

The perfect staining rag is a lint-free, white cotton T-shirt type material. It should be big enough to hold enough stain to do a three foot square area, but small enough to hold in the palm of your hand. Bigger rags will flop around and get stain everywhere you don't want it.

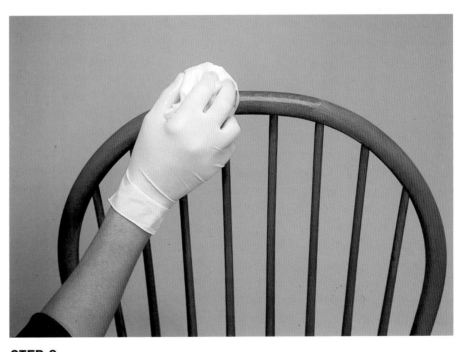

STEP 9
Apply the First Coat of Finish (15 minutes)

After the stain dries (this stain dries in an hour, but I always try to let stains sit overnight), apply the first coat of satin Varathane finish. This coat is really going to soak in quickly. An easy way to get the first coat on the rungs and spindles is to take a nylon cloth that is saturated with finish and rub it on. Work as quickly as you can—don't let the rag stick in any one place. Look back over your work as you go to catch any drips or runs before they start to set up.

STEP 14
Wipe the Glaze (10 minutes)

When you wipe, just wipe the high spots, letting more of the glaze stay in the grooves of the turnings.

STEP 15
Glazing the Seat (5 minutes)

To make the job easier, I first applied the glaze around the rungs on the seat. Try not to let the glaze pool up or drip on to the edge of the chair.

STEP 16
Wiping the Seat
On the chair seat, wipe the front and center of the seat clean, so it imitates natural aging from use. Let the glaze dry overnight and apply another coat of Varathane.

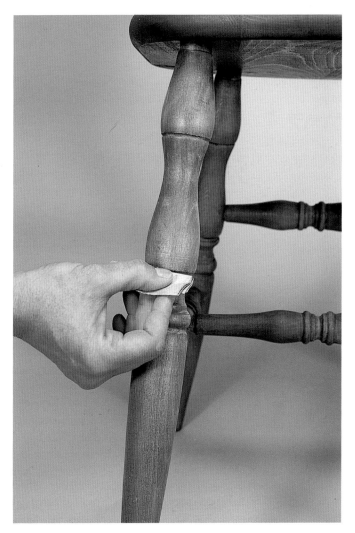

STEP 17
Finish the Chair (30 minutes)
Sand the finish with 400-grit sandpaper. This is the final sanding, so you want the surface to be as smooth and defect-free as possible. Fold a quarter sheet of sandpaper into fourths for a good edge to work in grooves. Wipe legs and rungs with a fine grit Scotchbrite.

It doesn't require a separate compressor and creates very little overspray. All spray systems—from spray cans to elaborate compressed air systems—work on the same basic principle. The finish is mixed in a solution that is placed under pressure and released from its container in a stream of air. HVLPs are very transfer efficient—they do a good job of getting the material you are spraying onto the surface instead of into the air and into your lungs. Even using a water-based finish and a HVLP you should still make sure you have good ventilation and wear a respirator.

Sprayed finishes have a lot of advantages over brushed finishes, even if toners aren't being used. There are no brush marks, it's much easier to get even coverage, and it's much faster.

You Need

- sandpaper—80-, 100-, 120-grit aluminum oxide, 400-grit silicon carbide, 600-grit wet/dry
- walnut water soluble aniline dye
- water borne finish
- HVLP system
- measuring cups
- gloves
- paint strainers
- tack cloth
- rags

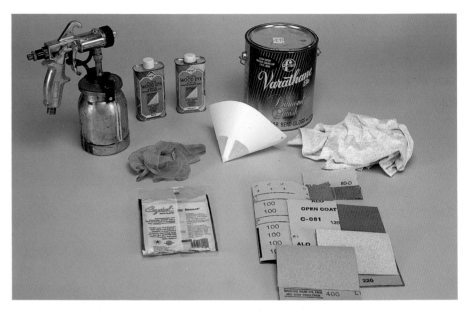

Curly maple has a beautiful, unique grain pattern that is subtly accented by a water-based toner.

KEYS TO SUCCESS

- Always keep your spray gun very clean. The tiniest particle can clog an air or fluid passage, distorting the spray pattern and creating an uneven finish.
- Straining the finish is very important. Small bits of dirt will travel right along with the finish and end up on your project—usually on what was going to be the final coat.
- Be sure to test spray the toner on a scrap piece of wood to check for strength of color. Once the toner is applied it is very hard to remove, especially if you use a quick drying finish. Water-based finishes look milky in the can and when sprayed preventing the true color from showing until the finish dries.

Step-by-Step Directions

STEP 1
Preparation (30 minutes)

After removing the lid and all hardware from the box, follow the preparation directions. Sand the entire box with 120-grit paper. Even though this curly maple is a highly figured wood, sand with the grain like any other wood.

STEP 2
Remove Burn Marks (2 minutes)

Burn marks from the router cut on the left corner molding of this box had to be sanded out with 80-grit paper. Re-sand any areas like that with 100 grit before the overall 120-grit sanding.

TIP

Don't skip grits on sandpaper. Sandpaper leaves scratches in the wood and each successive sanding has to remove the scratches of the previous grit. It's too much to expect 120 grit to remove the scratches left by 80 grit. It may seem like extra work, but in the long run it saves time and energy to sand with 100 grit in between. Water-based finishes seem to wear down sandpaper very quickly. Once a piece of sandpaper starts changing color because the grit is being rubbed off, it's time for a new piece. This project used a quarter sheet of 80 grit, a quarter sheet of 100 grit, one sheet of 120 grit, one sheet of 150 grit, one sheet of 220 grit, two sheets of 400 grit, and a half sheet of 600 grit.

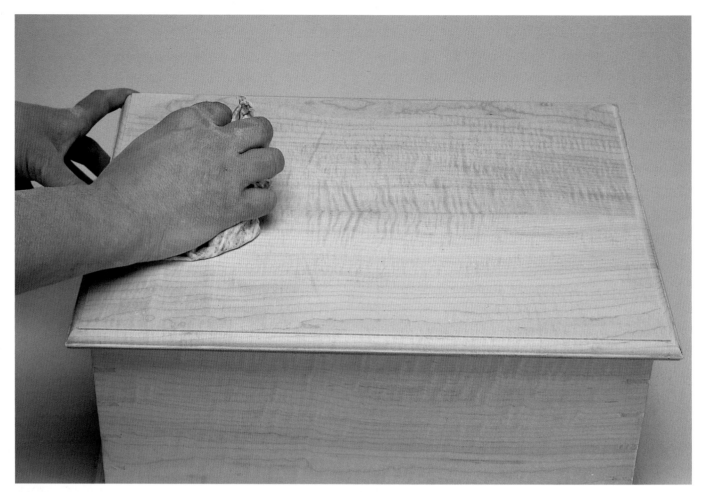

STEP 3
Raise the Grain (15 minutes)
Since water-based finishes raise the grain of the wood more than lacquer or oil-based varnishes, it helps to wet down the entire surface before the first coat of finish. After it dries, sand the wood with 150 grit to knock down the wood fibers.

STEP 4
First Steps to Spraying (1 minute)
Strain the finish into a quart cup and spray a coat on the bottom of the box and lid. (See sidebar on adjusting the spray gun on page 84.) Let these surfaces dry thoroughly before turning them over. Place the box on sticks or blocks to keep it raised above the surface of the spray table. This makes spraying the bottom edge much easier and lessens the risk of your project sticking to the table.

STEP 5
Spray the Inside (5 minutes)

Spray the inside of the box first. Narrow the fan on your spray gun and use caution when spraying into corners. Multiple light coats are better than one heavy coat that sags or runs. Then spray the outside of the box.

STEP 6
Spray the Edges (1 minute)

When spraying the lid of the box, first coat all four edges, then the top. This keeps the overspray from the edges from hitting the freshly sprayed top.

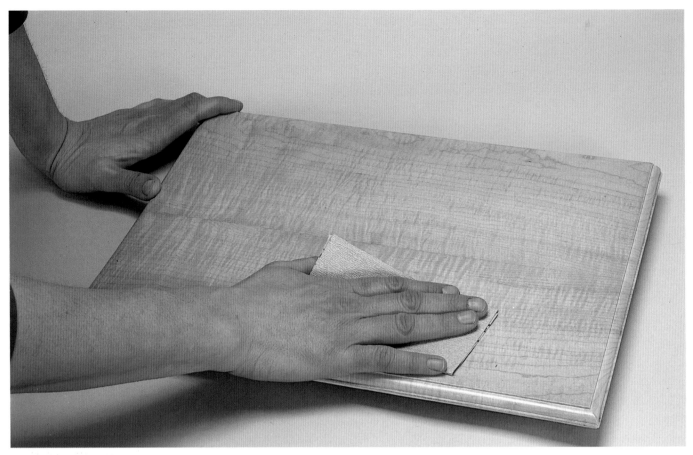

STEP 7
Sand Between Coats (15 minutes)
Most water-based finishes can be sanded and re-coated in two to three hours. Check the manufacturer's recommendations. Sand all surfaces with 220-grit paper and wipe off the sanding residue with a tack cloth.

High Volume, Low Pressure

An HVLP spray system is a great investment for the "home" finisher. These systems put out very little overspray so they are much neater and safer. An exhaust fan and filters should still be used. These need not be as elaborate as those required for compressed air systems, especially if you spray nonflammable finishes. The units can be run off standard household electricity. Some are also able to run off air compressors.

This clear gun shows the different channels finish goes through before it leaves the gun. The knob on the top controls the width of the spray pattern. The bottom knob controls the amount of material released. Air goes into the fitting at the bottom of the handle. The fluid enters the fitting in front of the trigger.

STEP 8
Smooth the Finish
Use even, gentle pressure when sanding, taking care not to sand all the way through the finish. You are just trying to smooth the finish by removing "nubbies."

STEP 9
Mix the Toner (2 minutes)
Add two tablespoons of dye to one quart of finish. If you want a stronger toner add more. Remember, the milkiness of water-based finishes really alters the color in the can and true color only shows after the finish has dried. Spray on an even coat on the bottoms of lid and box. Let dry before proceeding.

STEP 10
Spray on the Toner (20 minutes)

Spray an even coat of toner on the rest of the box. It is important to always keep your spray gun the same distance from the piece and moving at a steady rate. Pull the trigger while the gun is several inches away from the piece and continue spraying until the gun is several inches past it. This assures that you get good coverage on the edges but not an excess of finish which could run or look darker.

Let the finish dry and *very* carefully sand with 400-grit paper. Keep in mind the finish you are sanding has dye in it—too aggressive a sand will burn through the color and leave a light spot.

STEP 11
Repairing Defects (10 minutes)

Sometimes defects don't show up until a couple coats of finish have been applied. Maple is especially prone to tearing out when it is being machined, creating pits in the wood. This top had some very noticeable pits once it reached this stage. Notice the gaps between the saw kerf and the splines used on the corners of this box.

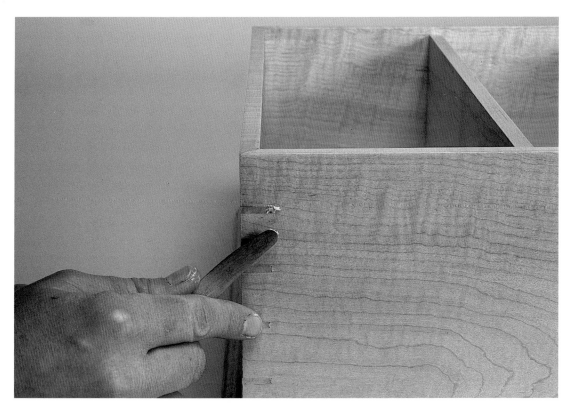

Apply Wax

Fill the gaps with a colored wax stick like this one available from Mohawk. They come in a variety of wood tones.

STEP 13
Trim Excess
Hold a straightedge razor perpendicular to the surface and gently scrape off the excess.

STEP 14
Polish Repair
Use a nylon scrubby pad to remove any remaining film. Make sure the wax stick you use is meant to be finished over.

STEP 15
Repaired Corner
This repair will be nearly invisible after the final coats of finish are applied.

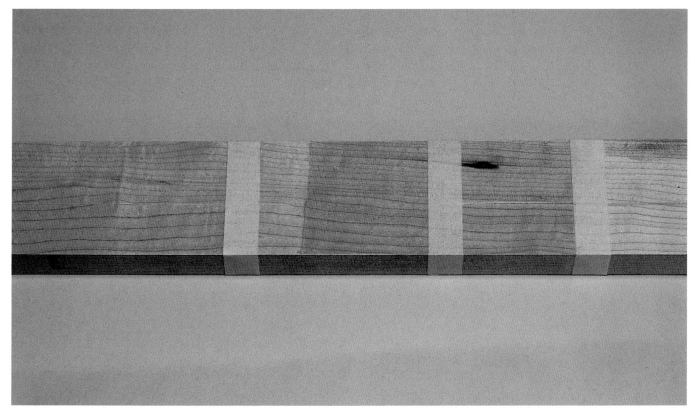

STEP 16
Spray the Final Coat (30 minutes)
Spray on another two coats of finish, sanding with 400 grit between coats. This board shows all the steps on this project. From left to right, notice the differences between the sections with a natural finish, the unfinished wood, the aniline dye toner, and the completely finished section. Finish out the box by wet sanding with 600 grit and rubbing with #0000 steel wool and polish.

Maintaining the Finish

IPN (interpenetrating polymer network) water-based finishes are very durable and resist scratching. They are best maintained by wiping with a barely damp cloth. Avoid any cleanser that contains ammonia. Vinegar and water works well on dirtier surfaces. Use a good grade of furniture polish that does not contain silicones. When the surface gets scratched, sand with 220-grit paper and re-coat.

Variations

This finish is easily duplicated using sprayed laquers or shellac. A water-based toner can also be brushed on, but it is difficult to get a perfectly even, brushstroke free application. Some varnishes and polyurethanes accept aniline dye and can be sprayed or brushed. Check the manufacturer's label and do a test piece first. Varnishes can be tinted with universal colorants to subtly alter the color of a project, but remember that universals are pigments, not dyes, and will not be as transparent.

CHAPTER 8

Classic Mahogany Finish on an Aspen Table

A brush-on lacquer is probably the most difficult finish to execute in this book. It is quick drying and can be unforgiveable in its application. Each layer melts back into the previous layer. While this creates outstanding adhesion between layers, it means each brushstroke must be light and carefully planned.

An advantage of a brush-on lacquer is that it closely duplicates the appearance and durability of a professionally sprayed lacquer. The difference between the two is that the solvents in a brushing lacquer are slightly slower drying than those of a spray. I use brushable lacquer when trying to match a finish where spraying isn't possible. With careful brushing and rubbing out of the final coat, it's hard to tell the difference.

Like spray lacquers, brush-on lacquers require strict safety precautions. The vapors are very flammable. They are heavier than air and collect at floor level, so make sure there are no pilot lights in your work area. Have plenty of ventilation and wear a respirator with an organic vapor cartridge.

You Need

- sandpaper—120-grit aluminum oxide, 220- and 400-grit silicon carbide
- red and brown aniline dye
- denatured alcohol
- shellac
- Guardsman's Warm Brown Glaze
- Park's Brushing Lacquer
- natural bristle brushes for glazing and finishing
- cotton rags
- gloves
- measuring cup, measuring spoons
- stir stick
- tack cloth

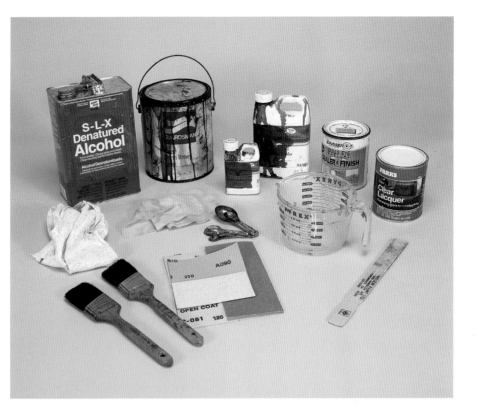

KEYS TO SUCCESS

- For a finished, professional look, stain and finish all surfaces that can possibly be seen—including underneath the table top and the back sides of table aprons.

- Resist the urge to go back into an area that is freshly lacquered—one small touch of the brush will eat through numerous layers of lacquer.

- Make sure your lacquering brush is in excellent condition and has soft bristles. Brushes with flagged bristles are best. The tips of these bristles have split ends that hold and release a lot of material and are very soft so they have less tendency to dig into the finish.

The depth and clarity of an aniline dye and glaze finish on this aspen table imitates the natural beauty of a much more expensive wood like mahogany. This finish turns inexpensive woods like aspen and poplar into beautiful pieces of furniture.

Step-by-Step Directions

STEP 1
Mix the Dye (20 minutes)

Aspen is a very light colored wood that doesn't absorb stain very well. To create the depth of this finish, a very strong dye is needed. Mix two tablespoons of red and two tablespoons of brown aniline dye with two cups of denatured alcohol.

STEP 2
Apply the Dye (10 minutes)

Apply the dye using a brush, rag or on large surfaces, a sponge. Work from bottom edges up so drips won't soak into raw wood.

STEP 3
Dye Large Surfaces (10 minutes)

Keep the sponge saturated with dye and apply in wet,
even overall strokes.

STEP 4
Dye Unassembled (30 minutes)

When possible, dye a piece of furniture before it's totally assembled. It's
much easier to dye a flat piece than to work into corners.

STEP 5
Let the Dye Dry (20 minutes)

As the dye dries, it will dramatically change colors. This dye turned a brilliant shade of pink. The color you should pay attention to is the wet dye color. This is one reason why it is very important to do a sample board first.

STEP 6
Sand the Dye (10 minutes)

Even though this dye is mixed in alcohol, the application was so wet that it raised the grain of the wood. Use 400-grit sandpaper to very lightly scuff the surface. This will remove the tips of the wood fibers that are sticking up. Be very careful around corners and edges because it is easy to sand through the color. If you sand through, carefully reapply some dye to the exposed area.

STEP 7
Apply the Shellac (20 minutes)

One of the secrets to creating a finish with a lot of depth is to isolate the layers of color. A barrier coat of shellac helps keep the colors from blending together into one color and is helpful on woods like aspen and poplar because they tend to accept stain or glaze unevenly. A coat of shellac will isolate the color and keep the glaze from soaking into the wood. Use a tack rag to remove the sanding dust—which in this case is very pink—and then apply a coat of shellac that has been cut in half with alcohol.

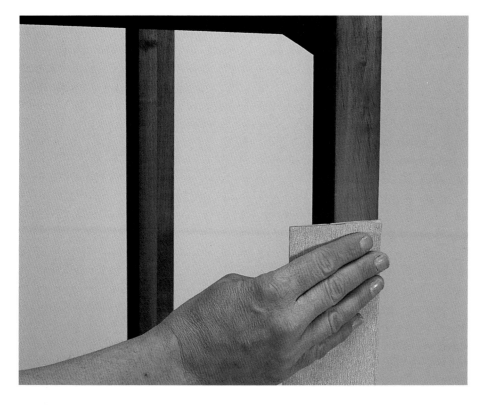

STEP 8
Sand the Shellac (10 minutes)

Allow the shellac to dry at least an hour and then lightly sand with 400-grit paper. Most of the shellac will have absorbed into the surface of the wood, so again, be extra careful sanding near edges. Avoid sanding through the dye. Your goal with this sanding is to get rid of any grit in the finish and provide a smooth surface for the glaze.

STEP 9
Apply the Glaze (15 minutes)

Use a brush to apply a wet coat of glaze—the technique is not important, but you do want to get 100 percent coverage. On a large surface, it's easier to apply the glaze with a rag. Be careful not to flick glaze on surfaces already glazed and wiped—it's just more mess to clean up. Glaze has a longer working time than a regular stain, but will start to set up in a couple minutes, so don't apply glaze to more surfaces than you can get to in less than five minutes. Large areas like desk tops or conference tables may require two people working as a team with one person applying and the other wiping.

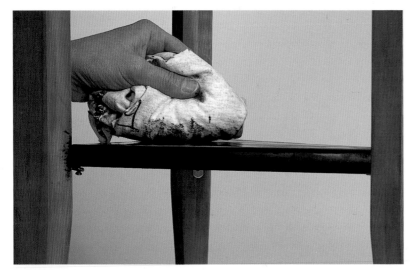

 TIPS
Nobody's perfect and chances are at some point you will get a run in your lacquer. Don't do anything! Let the run dry completely and then scrape the excess away with a sharp razor blade, sand the area with 400-grit paper and re-coat.

STEP 10
Wipe the Glaze (20 minutes)

Use a clean, lint-free cotton rag to wipe off the glaze. How much glaze to wipe off is a personal choice. A clean wipe will just barely color the wood and accent carvings and grooves. Leaving more glaze on will create a darker finish and begin to block out the color of the wood.

STEP 11
Blending With Glaze
Since this table is made from many small pieces of aspen that were not matched well in color, I left the glaze on rather heavy to blend the different pieces together.

STEP 12
Brush out the Glaze (5 minutes)
A light brushing with a dry natural bristle brush will soften any wiping marks left by the rag and clean up corner joints.

STEP 13
Brush on the Lacquer (20 minutes)

Allow the glaze to dry at least 24 hours. You should not be able to smell any solvent odor when it is dry. Dip a soft natural bristle brush into the lacquer and apply using quick, just barely overlapping strokes. Re-load your brush with lacquer frequently.

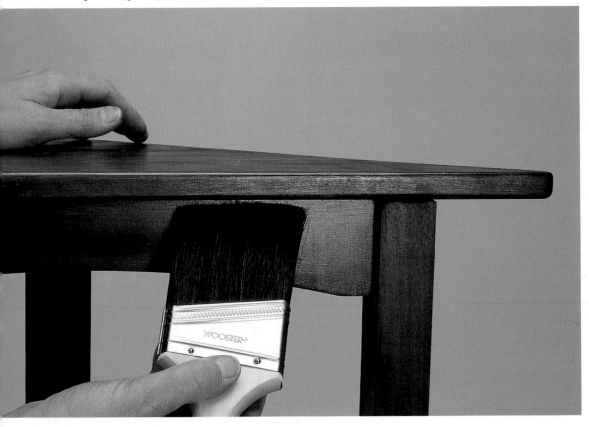

STEP 14
Brushing the Apron

Brushing lacquer requires a different technique than brushing an oil varnish. To brush the apron, place the brush at the top edge and pull down quickly. Do not attempt to rebrush with the grain.

STEP 15
Brushing the Legs

Start at the top of the legs and pull down with one continuous stroke. Do not go back over any surface that has wet lacquer on it. This will eat right through the lacquer and down to the aniline dye. Don't try to fix any mistakes now; any spots you miss will be caught on the next application.

STEP 16
The Finish Coats (1 hour)

⬤ Apply two more coats of lacquer without sanding between coats. Allow at least an hour drying time between coats. Then sand with 400-grit paper before the final coat. To imitate the look and feel of a sprayed lacquer finish you will almost certainly have to rub out the table. It's best to sand with 800-grit wet/dry paper dipped in soapy water and follow up by rubbing the finish with #0000 steel wool and a lubricant like Mohawk's Wool Lube.

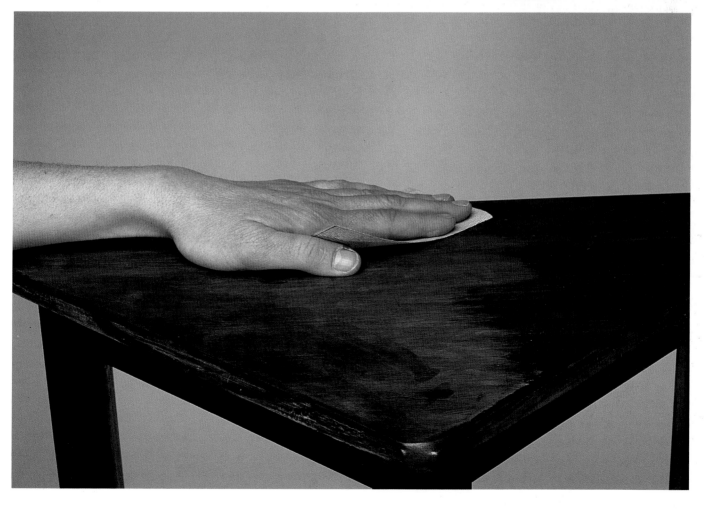

Next to safety and proper filtering of spray operations, dealing with waste is a major concern for home or small shop finishers. Large finishing operations collect their waste in drums and pay to have it hauled away and recycled. This is not practical for someone who only creates a small amount of waste. So what do you do?

The worst choice is to dump the waste down the drain. Do not ever do this! It is dangerous for you and for the water supply. Pouring the waste into the ground is also a very bad choice because it contaminates the ground. It might be tempting to think that a cup of mineral spirits isn't going to hurt anything, but those cups add up.

One acceptable solution is to place the waste in an open can and let the solvents evaporate. The solids can then be thrown out with your trash. I strongly discourage this because it adds to our air pollution.

The best way to deal with waste is to save it in a closed container. Almost all communities have waste collection days when you can turn in cans of waste for recycling. It is also a good time to clean your shelves of the old cans of stain, varnish and paint that have started to dry out, or that you know you're never going to use.

Check with your local city or county government for collection days. Do your part to make our environment healthier!

Maintaining the Finish

Brushed lacquers have the same durabilty as sprayed lacquers but are not nearly as strong as catalyzed finishes. Be very careful of fingernail polish remover and perfume. If either of these comes into contact with lacquer the finish will dissolve. Sometimes the dissolved area can be rubbed out, but more often than not, the entire surface must be refinished.

Variations

If spray equipment is available, this multi-stepped finish is much easier to complete. Many different finishes can be used with beautiful results—conventional lacquers, water-based varnishes or oil-based varnishes. Lacquer will dry the quickest and will trap less dust in the finish.

CHAPTER 9

Traditional Milk Paint Finish on a Pine Armoire

Milk paint is a time honored finish that became popular because of ease of application, availability of materials and durability of finish. Its popularity is resurging for the same reasons and because nothing else can as accurately recreate the gently worn look of an old painted piece.

Historically, milk paint was actually made from milk, lime and earth pigments. Milk contains casein which can be separated out to make paint and glue. Casein paint is one of the most durable kinds of paint. Today, milk paint can be bought in a powdered form and is easily mixed.

One positive aspect of milk paint is that it's nontoxic. It is a very strong finish, but it does easily spot from water, so any surface that might be exposed to water should be protected with a coat of wax or oil.

The first decision you have to make with milk paint is how opaque a finish you want. Milk paint can be applied in a water-thin concentration that will just barely color the wood, allowing most of the grain to show through. Or it can be applied in thick (about the consistency of a typical latex paint), multiple coats to a totally opaque painted finish allowing none of the grain to show. You may want to prepare a step board so you can see for yourself the effect of different consistencies and multiple coats.

The next decision is how smooth you want the piece to feel and look. Since milk paint is water based, it definitely raises the grain of the wood. Sanding between coats with 400-grit stearated paper or rubbing with a fine Scotchbrite nylon pad will give a smoother texture. Steel wool is not recommended because of its oil content and the danger of leaving small metal filings that will rust with the application of another coat of paint.

Now decide how you want to finish off the piece. Milk paint is durable but it does spot easily from water. For many applications, this is not a problem and the spotting only adds to the antiquity of the piece. The raw milk paint finish has a beautiful powdery look and feel that is hard to duplicate.

If you decide to seal the surface, be warned that most sealers significantly darken the color.

This custom built TV/stereo cabinet was designed to look like an old piece of country furniture. The milk paint finish was chosen to create an old, time-worn look.

KEYS TO SUCCESS

❧ Always keep paint, stain or finish thoroughly mixed. Stir every fifteen minutes to prevent separation of ingredients. This is especially true of milk paint you mix from a powder—it settles out quickly. If you don't keep the paint stirred, you'll have an increasingly weaker color as you go.

❧ Whenever you are mixing a color, make up enough to do the whole job. No matter how carefully you measure and keep records, it is very difficult to exactly re-match a color. This is a little tricky with milk paint, because once mixed it can only be stored in the refrigerator for a couple days. A quart of mixed paint is plenty to apply two coats of paint to this cabinet.

❧ Decide ahead of time which surfaces are going to be painted and carefully mask off those that are going to be left natural. Neatness definitely counts in finishing!

You Need

- powdered milk paint
- water
- strainer
- measuring cups
- sandpaper—120 grit
- brushes (nylon bristle and sponge)
- wire wisk
- universal colorant (optional)
- stir stick
- sanding block
- spray shellac
- paste wax
- cotton rag
- mixing bowl, plastic bucket

Step-by-Step Directions

STEP 1
Preparation (2 hours)

●● Sand the piece with 120-grit paper. Folding the paper into quarters makes it easier to get into grooves. Follow the directions listed in the preparation chapter. Even though this is a semi-opaque finish, sanding and preparation flaws will show through. This is a good finish to put on distressed wood to give it a more antique look.

 TIPS
If you are using a water-based system or dye, wet the wood, let it dry and scuff sand with 240-grit paper. This will cut off the raised fibers and help eliminate later grain raising.

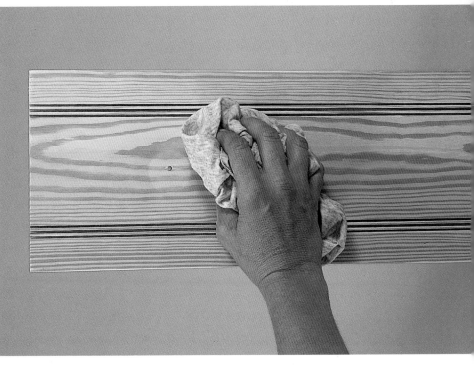

STEP 2
Prepare the Wood for Paint (20 minutes)

◔ Wet down the wood with a damp cloth. This raises the grain and helps assure even absorption of the paint.

STEP 3
Seal Knots (5 minutes)

Seal any knots with shellac to prevent bleeding (the color that comes through a knot). A spray can of shellac works great for this application. Use caution when spraying any finish—make sure you have a good supply of fresh air. Spray on light coats of finish.

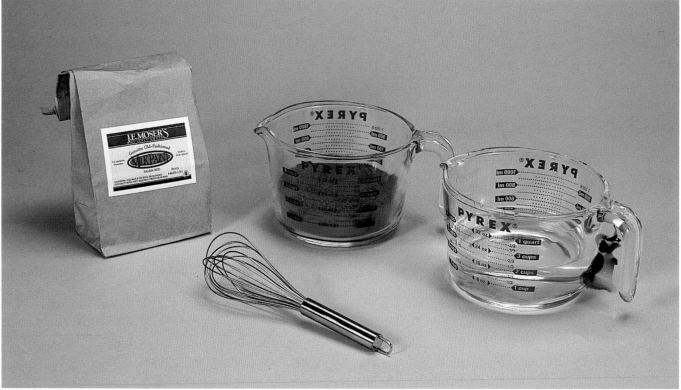

STEP 4
Using Powdered Milk Paint (2 minutes)

Follow the manufacturer's directions for preparing the milk paint. Some come premixed and some come in powdered form. The directions I'm giving are for a powder. Measure out equal parts of water and the paint powder. Warm water works best.

STEP 5
Mixing the Paint (5 minutes)

Pour the powder into the water, stirring as you add. For a more opaque finish, use more powder. For a more transparent stain, use less.

STEP 6
Stir the Paint (5 minutes)

Thoroughly stir the mixture. I use a wire whisk—you can also use an egg beater or electric mixer. Depending on the size of your batch, you need to keep stirring for two to three minutes. All the dry powder should be mixed in and the paint should be smooth.

STEP 7
Strain the Paint (1 minute)

Strain the paint through a strainer or cheesecloth to remove any remaining lumps. Clean all your tools right away—once milk paint dries, it is almost impossible to remove—as many a refinisher will verify!

STEP 8
Tint the Paint (2 minutes)

Milk paint can be tinted either by intermixing colors of paint or by adding a small amount of a universal colorant compatible with water-based paints. Cal-tint and Mixol are two examples. I needed mine to be a deeper red, so I added some bright red colorant. Remember, these colorants are very concentrated, so only add a couple of drops at a time.

STEP 9
Apply the Paint to Grooves (15 minutes)

After letting the paint sit for ten minutes, use a nylon brush to apply paint in the grooves. These grooves are really deep and I had to work the brush back and forth to get total coverage. Always paint grooves and carvings first because you want the big surface to have the smoothest strokes.

STEP 10
Paint the Edges (5 minutes)

Paint the edges next. I used a foam brush because it is easy to control. Bristle brushes tend to splay out and get paint on the back side.

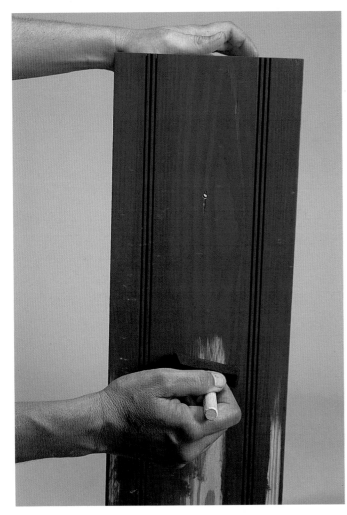

STEP 11
Paint Flat Surfaces (30 minutes)

Paint the rest of the drawer. Again, the sponge brush works well because it doesn't leave brush marks. The paint might look a little streaky, but that's a characteristic of milk paint.

STEP 12
Remove the Excess Paint (30 minutes)

Unless you're a lot neater than I am, there's probably paint built up in the grooves. Take a dry brush and clean them out. Shove the excess paint to the end of the drawer and catch it with a cloth so it doesn't get all over the drawer box. Since I wanted a fairly transparent finish, I wiped the drawer down with a dry rag to remove any excess paint. I got heavy handed with one drawer so I had to reapply some paint.

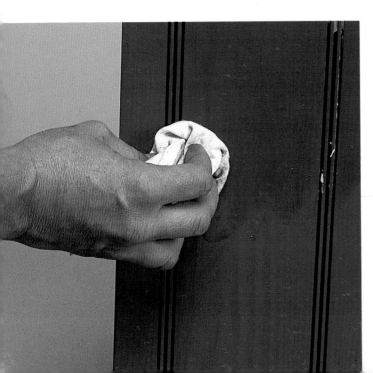

STEP 13
Wax (1 hour)

Let the piece dry overnight and apply paste wax if desired. Put the wax on in a thin but even coat. Immediately remove any excess wax that gets into the grooves. After the wax is dry—about 20 minutes—buff the surface with a soft cotton cloth. This photo shows how much the wax darkens the color of milk paint.

Antiquing Brass Knobs

Most inexpensive brass plated knobs are very shiny and new looking. There are many ways to age them to make them look "fake antique." The simplest is to apply a glaze or stain.

STEP 1
Apply the Glaze
Use a soft natural bristle brush to apply the glaze to the knobs. Don't drown them, but be sure to get glaze into the grooves.

STEP 2
Wipe off the Glaze
With a soft cotton rag, wipe off the high spots of the knobs. Leave some glaze down in the grooves to re-create the look of hundreds of years of use. For a more subtle contrast between high and low surfaces, gently dab the knob with a brush after you wipe it.

STEP 3
Seal the Knobs
Let the glaze dry overnight. Spray the knobs with a coat of shellac, lacquer or varnish. An aerosol can works great for this.

Maintaining the Finish

One advantage of an antiqued finish is it only gets older looking with use. Left on its own, milkpaint will develop a natural patina combining dull with shiny areas. Even though the finish is very strong, water will spot it. If you find these spots objectionable, you should apply a coat of wax. Occasional spots that detract from the beauty of the finish can be rubbed out with #0000 steel wool.

Stripping and Refinishing an Antique Walnut Cabinet

There aren't many things as rewarding as unleashing the beauty of a piece of furniture that has been hidden under multiple coats of paint. Before you choose a piece of furniture to refinish there are a number of questions to answer. Does the piece need to be refinished or just cleaned up? Is the piece worth the time and effort refinishing takes? Will any antique value of the piece be lost if it is refinished?

Antique value aside, refinishing versus cleaning is an aesthetic decision if the finish is in basically good shape. If there are serious flaws in the finish, it should come off. However, if the finish is just dull, slightly scratched or lifeless, a good cleaning with TSP (trisodium phosphate) and a coat of wax or new finish may be all that is needed.

When choosing a piece for refinishing you have to be a bit of a detective. Check the joinery to determine how well the piece was made. Dovetail joints are usually a sign that a piece is well made and worthy of refinishing. Staples and particleboard usually indicate that the furniture is not of very high quality. Unless you have x-ray vision, it can be very difficult to determine what kind of wood is underneath layers of paint. Check the inside of drawer fronts or the underneath sides of table tops and hope the painter wasn't

overly efficient. If you can't find any unpainted surface, strip a small spot in an inconspicuous area before you tackle the whole project.

If the furniture you're considering refinishing has its original finish and is a true antique, take it to a professional furniture restorer. Removing the original finish could greatly diminish its antique value.

You Need

- stripper
- medium nylon scrub pad
- dust mask
- plastic bucket
- old natural bristle brush
- putty knife
- stiff nylon bristle scrub brush
- trisodium phosphate
- oxalic acid
- synthetic sponge
- sandpaper—80, 100, 120, 220, 400 grits
- stir stick
- wood putty
- wood epoxy putty
- cotton rags
- shellac
- natural bristle brush
- #0000 steel wool
- paste wax
- strainer
- denatured alcohol

- safety glasses
- gloves
- tack rag
- spray lacquer toner
- sanding block
- touch up powders
- touch up liquid
- wax stick
- touch up brush

A little time and effort transformed this walnut cabinet from its 1960s antiquing kit finish to its natural walnut beauty.

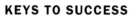

KEYS TO SUCCESS

- If you are stripping a vertical surface, make sure you use a heavy bodied stripper. These have a higher wax content and cling better to the surface, allowing the stripper to work more effectively.

- Let the chemical do the work. Once stripper is applied, a barrier forms on the surface that keeps the stripper underneath from evaporating. It's hard to avoid the temptation of "messing" with the stripper, but it just makes for more work in the long run. On large surfaces or very hot days it helps to put a sheet of heavy-duty plastic over the stripper to create an even stronger barrier.

- But moderation in all things. The chemicals in the stripper can literally burn the wood, so be careful not to leave it on longer than necessary.

Step-by-Step Directions

STEP 1
Apply the Stripper (20 minutes)

Remove all hardware from the piece of furniture. Find a safe place to strip—plenty of ventilation, out of direct sunlight, away from pilot lights, and far enough away from anything you don't want stripper splashed on. Protect your work surface with heavy plastic. Stripping is messy. Have a bucket of clean water close at hand in case you get any stripper on yourself. Put on your gloves, wear long sleeves, and *put on your safety goggles!* One tiny pinhead-sized speck of stripper in your eye will cause excruciating pain and probably a trip to the emergency room. Experience speaks.

Pour stripper into a heavy bucket or other container. With a fully loaded brush, dab on the stripper. Re-load your brush frequently and do not try to brush out the stripper. A thin coat of stripper will evaporate before it has time to remove the finish. Remember, a barrier film forms almost immediately and you do not want to disturb it. If an area dries up quickly, re-apply stripper to that spot.

STEP 2
Take a Break (15 minutes)

Let the stripper do the work. The paint will begin wrinkling and eventually bubble up. Test a small area with a putty knife to see if the finish has been removed down to the bare wood. Some paints can only be removed one layer at a time. If the top layers are completely bubbled up, but nothing seems to be happening beneath them, proceed to the next step.

STEP 3
Scrape off the Finish (15 minutes)

Carefully remove the layers of finish that have bubbled up. Do not try to force any finish off that is not loose—you run the risk of gouging the wood. Place the stripping residue in a separate container.

STEP 4
Apply the Second Coat of Stripper (15 minutes)

Sometimes one coat of stripper is enough, but I almost always do at least two applications to make sure all the finish has been completely removed. Apply the second coat as the first.

STEP 5
Scrub the Stripper (10 minutes)

After the reapplication starts to work, scrub the stripper with a stiff bristle brush or nylon scrubby pad. This works the finish out of the grain of the wood, corners and carvings.

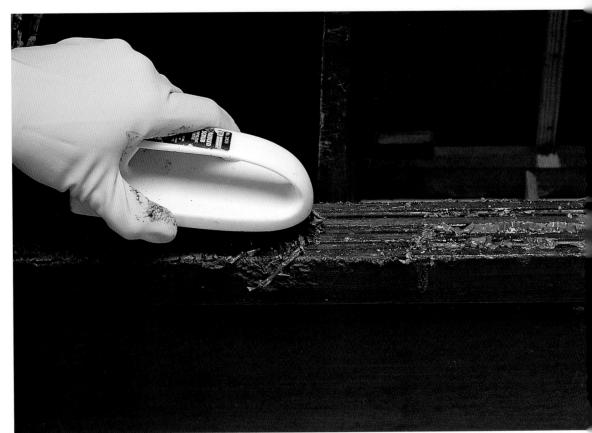

STEP 6
Rinse With TSP (10 minutes)

Mix a half cup of TSP (trisodium phosphate—a non-sudsing soap available at paint stores) in hot water and apply to the surface with a stiff brush or scrubby pad. Work it vigorously into the wood. Remove excess liquid with a sponge, then rinse with clean water. Immediately wipe as dry as possible.

STEP 7
Lighten Wood (5 minutes)

Often the process of chemically stripping wood leaves it with a gray appearance. Oak can turn almost black. To counteract this, rinse the piece in a solution of oxalic acid (one cup of oxalic to one gallon of hot water). On vertical surfaces, apply the acid from the bottom up to prevent drip marks. Let the solution dry and then *thoroughly rinse with clean water*. The dried oxalic acid dust is very irritating and will burn your nasal passages when you sand the piece if it is not completely washed off.

STEP 8
Let Dry (12 hours)

Let your piece of furniture dry overnight before proceeding with the prep work. Notice how light and evenly colored the wood is after drying.

STEP 9
Filling Open Joints (15 minutes)

Stripping an old finish off will probably reveal damaged areas that may not have shown under layers of paint. The joints of the solid wood top underlayment were open. I filled the joints with wood putty and let them dry.

STEP 10
Finishing Repair (10 minutes)

Sand smooth with 80-grit paper. Make sure all excess putty is sanded off.

STEP 11
Damaged Veneer
The bottom apron of this cabinet was very damaged. The veneer was loose and a large piece was missing.

STEP 12
Clean out Glue Area (2 minutes)
In order for the veneer to be re-glued, all stripping residue, dust and old glue had to be thoroughly cleaned out. Use a folded piece of sand-paper to scrape the area between the veneer layers clean.

STEP 13
Apply the Glue (5 minutes)

To get into the tight space between the layers of veneer, apply some carpenter's glue to the end of a thin putty knife. Carefully lift the veneer and scrape the glue into the space.

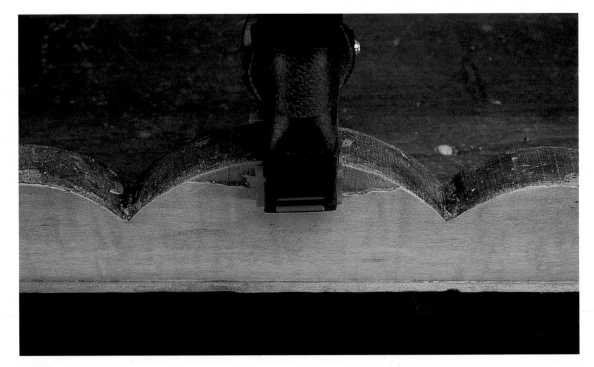

STEP 14
Clamp and Let Dry (30 minutes)

If possible, clamp the veneer until the glue dries. On some edges a piece of masking tape is enough to hold down the loose veneer.

STEP 15
Replace the Missing Veneer (5 minutes)

Missing veneer can be replaced with another piece of veneer carefully cut out and glued in place. A simpler alternative is to fill the void with a two part wood epoxy putty. First scrape the area clean. Mix the epoxy according to package directions and press the putty into the hole. When the putty hardens to the consistency of an apple, take a straightedge razor blade and shave off the excess. Let the putty thoroughly harden and then sand with 80-grit paper. The epoxy will accept some stain, but will also have to be colored in to match the surrounding veneer.

Touch up Damaged Areas

Many defects in furniture can be cosmetically hidden using materials available from paint stores or catalogues. Mohawk, Star and Behlen's all have numerous products that are easy to use and that hide a multitude of sins.

A colored wax stick can be rubbed in to small nicks and chips. Scrape the excess away with a razor blade or the edge of a credit card. Spray toners can be used to add a little color to wood that doesn't quite match.

More detailed cosmetic repair can be done by using powdered colors. A small amount of pigment is mixed with a shellac-like solvent and applied with a small detail brush. First paint in the background color of the wood and then add the tiny grain lines.

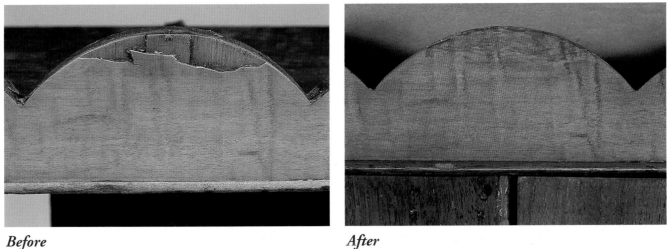

Before
After

STEP 16
Sand the Piece and Apply Shellac (50 minutes)

At this point the preparation for a refinishing process is the same as for a new finishing project. Begin sanding with 80 grit, followed by 100 and 120. Be sure to wear a dust mask to prevent irritation from any remaining oxalic acid. In spite of the layers of paint, this walnut piece still had a beautiful color, so I decided to use a natural shellac finish. Remove any sanding dust from the piece with an old paint brush or pressurized air. Dip a natural bristle brush about two-thirds of the way into the shellac. Apply the shellac with long flowing motions, trying not to overlap or brush back into already shellacked surfaces.

STEP 17
Tone the Edges (5 minutes)

The area that was test-stripped showed this cabinet was made from walnut. What it didn't show was the solid wood structural pieces were poplar. To blend the poplar pieces with the walnut, mask them off and spray with an aerosol lacquer toner. Use very light coats, building slowly to the desired color.

TIPS

Don't try to skip grits on sanding. If you start with 80 grit, go next to 100, then to 120. At each step, you should get rid of any of the sanding scratches left by the previous grit. Often you should machine sand with one grit finer than what you want your final sanding to be. The machine is much more aggressive than you are so be sure to compensate for it. Always finish up by sanding by hand. It's the only way you can know for sure that all of the sanding marks are straight and with the grain of the wood.

STEP 18
Apply the Finish Coats (15 minutes)

Let the shellac dry a couple hours, sand with 220-grit paper, tack off sanding dust, and re-coat. Remember, a light, quick touch is very important with shellac. Never let your brush stop on the surface or it will dissolve previous layers of shellac. When the final layer is dry, a quick rub with #0000 steel wool and a coat of paste wax will even out the sheen and provide added protection from water.

Color Matching

Matching color can be very hard and frustrating for the beginning finisher. It gets easier with experience, especially if sample boards are labelled and saved. Use them as a reference—don't reinvent the wheel with every new project.

The first step in successful color matching is to isolate the colors. Look closely at what you are trying to match. Finished wood is a combination of different colors arranged in layers. No one color is ever going to duplicate the appearance of the transluscent layers found in many finished woods.

Look for the lightest color in the wood. This is usually found in the hardest part of the wood and, on carved pieces, will be along the top edges. You can get an indication of what the new piece will look like with a clear coat of finish by wetting a portion with mineral spirits. You can compare the light and the dark areas of the new piece with the existing piece to determine whether you need to color the new finish. If the colors of the two woods are similar, you probably don't need a dye. But if you are trying to match an older piece, a high-end manufactured piece, or woods of two different species, using a dye will probably make your color matching a lot easier. To imitate the golden glow of old walnut, use a yellow-orange dye. To blend a new walnut piece with a traditionally finished dark red mahogany piece, use a red dye. Go one step stronger with the dye than you want the final color to be. It will be toned down by subsequent stains or glazes.

Next look at the wood pore—the tiny straight holes in the wood. If it's filled, use a pigmented filler to

duplicate the color. If it's not filled, the glaze or stain will color it for you—usually a shade darker than the overall color.

This may be all the coloring you need. Apply a thin coat of finish to your sample board and check it against what you are trying to match. Shellac generally works well as this thin, or wash, coat.

The third layer of color to match is the overall color that is much closer to the surface. Imagine looking through a sheet of tinted cellophane. This color can be achieved with a stain, glaze or toner. See chapter four for an explanation of the differences between the three.

It is possible to sometimes take a can of stain off the shelf and get exactly the color you want. Stains also can be intermixed as long as they are the same kind—oil with oil, gel with gel or water with water. But for consistent success with color matching, it really is easier to go through the extra steps of layering your color. The results will be much more pleasing.

Quick Reference Chart

This chart contains generalizations about stains and finishes. Be sure to check the following manufacturer's recommendations.

FINISH	SOLVENT	DRYTIME	CHARACTERISTICS
aniline dye	alcohol	10 minutes	transparent, fairly deep penetration, very quick drying
aniline dye	water	1 hour depending on humidity	transparent, deepest penetration, slower drying than alcohol
wiping stains and oil glazes	mineral spirits	12 hours	easy to apply, slightly opaque, fair penetration
Danish oil	mineral spirits	24 hours	rubbed into wood, no surface film forms
water-based stains	water	1 hour depending on humidity	good penetration, raises grain
shellac	alcohol	15 minute touch, 2 hours re-coat	excellent clarity, white (clear) shellac is slightly amber, orange (amber) is very amber, good durability, but susceptible to water and alcohol
oil varnish	mineral spirits	2 hours dust free, 12 hours re-coat	easily brushed, good clarity, slightly amber, yellows with age, good durability
oil polyurethane	mineral spirits	2 hours dust free, 12 hours re-coat	a little harder to brush than varnish, amber color
water-based finishes	water/alcohol	20 minute to touch, 3 hours re-coat	dries very clear, slightly difficult to brush, newest IPN and polys are very durable
nitrocellulose lacquer	lacquer thinner	5 minute touch, 15 minute re-coat	very quick drying, slightly amber, excellent clarity, good durability
catalyzed lacquer and varnish	lacquer thinner toluol	5 minute touch, 15 minute re-coat	very quick drying, outstanding durability, good clarity

APPLICATION	COMPATIBILITY	NOTES
most easily sprayed	fully compatible	can be added to shellac or lacquer to make a transparent toner
spray, sponge brush, rag	fully compatible with thorough drying	can be added to water-based finish to make transparent toner
wipe or brush on, rag off	very safe under lacquers and oil varnishes—can be used under water-based with thorough drying time	will often look splotchy on some woods, should be wiped clean to reduce opacity
brush and rag	can be coated with oil varnish or lacquer after thoroughly dry, do not use on top of any finish	be very careful with soiled rags—place in water
polyester or foam brush, rag	full compatibility when thoroughly dry	should be sanded before finishing
spray, natural bristle brush, rag	compatible as sealer coat with just about everything	beautiful finish on its own, excellent barrier coat, nontoxic
spray or natural bristle brush	cannot be topcoated with lacquer	slow drying, may trap dust in finish that has to be rubbed out
spray or natural bristle brush	do not use on top of any finish with stearates	
polyester or sponge brush, spray	oil stains and finishes must be thoroughly dry, recommended over lacquer	the finish of the future, nontoxic, low fume
spray, a few can be brushed	use on top of oil and water stains with proper drying, good on top of shellac, don't use on top of oil finishes	flammable, wear respirator, use spray booth
spray only	use on top of oil and water stains, don't use on top of anything except vinyl sealer	flammable, wear respirator, the strongest of finishes in the book, but also the most hazardous

Glossary

ADHESION—How well a layer of finish sticks to the layer below it or to the piece being finished.

ALKYD—A synthetic resin added to finishes to increase hardness and durability.

ANILINE DYE—A transparent dye used in wood finishing; may be soluble in alcohol water and other liquids; comes in powdered form or pre-dissolved.

BARRIER COAT—A layer of finish applied to separate layers of color or the finish from the substrate.

BINDER—The film-forming part of a finish—what's left besides the pigment when the solvents evaporate.

BLEEDING—When a color from a lower layer leeches through to an upper layer of finish.

CATALYZED—A finish that has a chemical additive that increases the rate of cure and hardness.

COMPATIBILITY—The ability of two finishes to be mixed together or used on top of each other.

CURE—The amount of time it takes a finish to totally dry and harden.

DANISH OIL—Usually tung or linseed oil thinned with mineral spirits and "toughened" with alkyd resins.

DENATURED ALCOHOL—The solvent used to thin shellac; a good solvent for aniline dyes.

END GRAIN—The cut of wood that slices through the grain—it will soak up stain and finish unless sealed off.

FILLER—A semi-paste material that is used to fill the pores of open-grain woods like oak and mahogany.

FILM—The layer of finish that is on top of the wood.

GLAZE—A color (either paint or pigment) that is suspended in oil or varnish so that it dries translucent. Compare with dye and stain.

GRAIN—The pattern created by the shape and arrangement of the cells in wood.

GRIT—The degree of abrasiveness in sandpaper and steel wool. With steel wool, the higher the number, the coarser the grit. Sandpaper is the opposite—the higher the number, the finer the grit.

HVLP—"High volume, low pressure"—a kind of spray equipment that gets the finish right on the wood instead of in the air.

IPN (INTERPENETRATING POLYMER NETWORK)—A crosslinked waterbourne polyurethane finish.

LACQUER THINNER—The solvent used for lacquers—very flammable and strong smelling.

MINERAL SPIRITS—The solvent used with oil-based varnishes and paint; commonly called paint thinner.

OPACITY—How easily you can see through something. Clear glass is transparent; tinted glass is translucent.

OVERSPRAY—The finish that goes into the air instead of on the piece being sprayed.

OXALIC ACID—A mild bleach for wood.

PIGMENT—Any mineral added to a finish—in this book, and in general use, a pigment is an opaque color.

POLYURETHANE—A fairly modern breed of finish, traditionally oil based, but now available in lacquers and water based.

PORE—The open part of the wood grain that gives some woods, like oak, an actual texture.

PUTTY—A very thick paste that is used to fill small holes in wood.

SEALER—A specially formulated finish that bonds well with raw wood and sands easily.

SET UP—The time it takes for a finish to dry to the touch.

SHADING STAIN—A finish with pigment added to it to add color, more opaque than a toner.

SHEEN—How shiny a finish is, rated on a scale of 1-100—dead flat is 5 or below, gloss is 75 or above.

SHELF LIFE—How long a finish is still usable in an unopened can. Shellac and pre-catalyzed finishes have limited shelf lives.

SOLUBLE—Capable of being dissolved by another substance.

SOLVENT—The liquid that evaporates when a finish dries—but just because a finish has a solvent in it doesn't mean it's soluble by that solvent. Eg., water-based finishes are not water soluble.

STAIN—An opaque pigment that is rubbed into wood—see aniline dye and toner.

STEARATED—Finish or sandpaper with a soft powder added that makes sanding easier.

TONER—A finish with a dye added to it for additional color.

TRISODIUM PHOSPHATE—A powdered, non-sudsing soap used for clean up in the final stages of stripping a finish.

UNIVERSAL COLORANTS—Pigments that can be added to most finishes.

Sources

Almost all of the materials used in the projects in this book can be purchased at your local hardware or paint store. For those without easy access to retail stores that carry finishing supplies, here's a list of suppliers and catalogues. Many companics are now also available on the Internet.

GUARDSMAN PRODUCTS—(910) 802-4500
Ask for local retail sources.

VARATHANE—(800) 635-3286
Call to find a local distributor—a wide range of products, including their excellent water-based Diamond Finish.

LIBERON—(800) 245-5611; www.liberon.com
A full line of finishing supplies, wonderful waxes.

MOHAWK FINISHING PRODUCTS—(800) 545-0047
Mohawk recently bought out Star Finishing Products and has one of the most extensive mail order finish supply operations. Their products are available in retail stores under the Behlen label. The catalogue is a great source of finishing tips.

WOODWORKER'S SUPPLY CATALOGUE—(800) 645-9292

CONSTANTINE'S—(800) 223-8087

VAN DYKE'S RESTORER'S CATALOGUE—(800) 558-1234

INDEX